QUESTIONS ABOUT GOD

QUESTIONS ABOUT GOD

Today's Philosophers
Ponder the Divine

Edited by
STEVEN M. CAHN
&
DAVID SHATZ

UNIVERSITY PRESS

2002

OXFORD

UNIVERSITY PRESS

Oxford   New York

Auckland   Bangkok   Buenos Aires   Cape Town   Chennai
Dar es Salaam   Delhi   Hong Kong   Istanbul   Karachi   Kolkata
Kuala Lumpur   Madrid   Melbourne   Mexico City   Mumbai   Nairobi
São Paulo   Shanghai   Singapore   Taipei   Tokyo   Toronto

and an associated company in Berlin

Published by Oxford University Press, Inc.,
198 Madison Avenue, New York, New York 10016

www.oup.com

Oxford is a registered trademark of Oxford University Press

Library of Congress Cataloging-in-Publication Data
Questions about God : today's philosophers ponder the Divine / edited by Steven M.
Cahn and David Shatz.
p. cm.
A collection of essays by leading philosophers previously published from 1973 to 1998.
Includes bibliographical references and index.
ISBN 0-19-515037-6; ISBN 0-19-515038-4 (pbk.)
1. God. 2. Theism. 3. Philosophical theology. 4. Philosophy, Modern—20th century.
I. Cahn, Steven M. II. Shatz, David
BT103.Q84   2004
211—dc21   2001053121

1 3 5 7 9 8 6 4 2

Printed in the United States of America
on acid-free paper

Assuming God exists, can the use of reason enable us to gain any insight into His nature? For example, do His commands need to conform to moral standards, or does He Himself set the standards? Is God's power limited in any way, or can He change the past or contravene the laws of logic? Why, if God is all good, does He allow catastrophes and atrocities? Is God obliged to make us happy, or is that expectation inappropriate? Why does God remain hidden and not provide stronger evidence of His presence? Is God vain, and if not, why does He expect to be worshiped? Why does God want us to pray, rather than grant what we deserve regardless of whether we ask for it? Whom does God consign to hell, and why is everlasting punishment for nonbelievers justified? Does God, witnessing the horrors of the world, suffer anguish, or is He an impassive observer of tragic events? Does God change, or is He eternally the same, regardless of the world's changing? Does God know our future choices, and if He does, are they nevertheless free? Do all religions worship the same god, and if so why do they describe the divinity differently?

These are the questions addressed in the essays collected here. The authors are noted contemporary philosophers, and their articles make clear that work in philosophy today is frequently sympathetic to theism. While current literature in the field is often highly technical, these articles are understandable by all, and they have been edited where appropriate to enhance accessibility. The positions defended are by no means beyond dispute. But the arguments offered are challenging and should provoke the sort of debate that is essential to philosophical inquiry. The authors display clarity, ingenuity, rigor, and intellectual honesty. Whether their conclusions are persuasive is for readers to decide.

The book does not assess the age-old arguments for the existence of God. These arguments are not the only provocative issues in philosophy of religion, and we have focused on other equally fascinating ones. For theists, as most of these authors are, understanding the nature and ways of God is obviously of utmost importance. For those who are not theists, the inquiry is nonetheless intellectually engaging and may test previously hidden assumptions regarding the theistic hypothesis.

To affirm the existence of God but not be able to understand anything at all about His ways may provide spiritual sustenance but is intellectually barren. These essays are the best attempts of contemporary philosophers to disclose aspects of the divine. What is revealed we leave to the reader's judgment.

We are grateful to Cynthia Read, our editor at Oxford University Press, for her advice and support. We also wish to express our appreciation to the staff of Oxford University Press for providing generous assistance throughout the stages of production. Finally, we thank Samuel Groner for preparing the index.

New York, New York   S. M. C.
April 2002   D. S.

ACKNOWLEDGMENTS

Chapter 1. From *The Elements of Moral Philosophy,* second edition, by James Rachels. Copyright © 1993 by McGraw-Hill. Reprinted by permission of The McGraw-Hill Corporation.

Chapter 2. Reprinted from *Philosophy 48* (1973) by permission of Cambridge University Press. © The Royal Institute of Philosophy, 1973.

Chapter 3. From *Is There a God?* Copyright © 1996 by Richard Swinburne. Reprinted by permission of Oxford University Press.

Chapter 4. From "Suffering and Evil," by George Schlesinger, in *Contemporary Philosophy of Religion,* eds. Steven M. Cahn and David Shatz. Copyright © 1982 by Oxford University Press. Reprinted by permission of the publisher.

Chapter 5. From the *American Philosophical Quarterly 30* (1993), reprinted by permission of the editor.

Chapter 6. From *Faith and Philosophy 6* (1989), reprinted by permission.

Chapter 7. From the *American Philosophical Quarterly 16* (1979), reprinted by permission of the editor.

Chapter 8. From *Modern Theology 6* (1990), © 1990 by Blackwell Publishers, Ltd. Reprinted by permission.

Chapter 9. From Nicholas Wolterstoff, "Suffering Love," in *Philosophy and the Christian Faith,* ed. Thomas J. Morris. © 1998 by University of Notre Dame Press. Reprinted by permission.

Chapter 10. From *The Openness of God,* by Clark Pinnock, Richard Rice, John Sanders, William Hasker, and David Basinger. Copyright © 1994. Reprinted by permission of InterVarsity Press and Paternoster Press.

Chapter 11. Published here for the first time. Copyright © 2002 by Steven M. Cahn.

Chapter 12. From John Hick, *God and the Universe of Faiths* (London: The Macmillan Press, Ltd., 1973). Copyright © 1973 Macmillan. Reprinted by permission.

CONTENTS

CONTRIBUTORS

Steven M. Cahn is professor of philosophy at the Graduate Center of the City University of New York.

Stephen T. Davis is professor of philosophy at Claremont Graduate University.

Peter Geach is professor of philosophy at the University of Cambridge in England.

William Hasker is professor of philosophy at Huntington College.

John Hick was professor of philosophy at Claremont Graduate University and is now a fellow at the University of Birmingham in England.

Michael J. Murray is associate professor of philosophy at Franklin and Marshall College.

James Rachels is professor of philosophy at the University of Alabama at Birmingham.

George N. Schlesinger is professor emeritus of philosophy at the University of North Carolina, Chapel Hill.

David Shatz is professor of philosophy at Yeshiva University.

Eleonore Stump is professor of philosophy at St. Louis University.

Richard Swinburne is professor of the Christian religion at Oxford University.

Charles Taliaferro is professor of philosophy at St. Olaf College.

Nicholas Wolterstorff is professor emeritus of philosophical theology at Yale University.

QUESTIONS ABOUT GOD

ONE

MUST GOD'S COMMANDS CONFORM TO MORAL STANDARDS?

James Rachels

In both the Jewish and Christian traditions, God is presented as a lawgiver who has created us, and the world we live in, for a purpose. That purpose is not completely understood, but much has been revealed through the prophets, the Holy Scriptures, and the church. These sources teach that, to guide us in righteous living, God has promulgated rules that we are to obey. He does not compel us to obey them. We were created as free agents, so we may choose to accept or to reject his commandments. But if we are to live as we *should* live, we must follow God's laws. This, it is said, is the essence of morality.

This line of thought has been elaborated by some theologians into a theory about the nature of right and wrong, known as the *Divine Command Theory*. Essentially, this theory says that "morally right" means "commanded by God," and "morally wrong" means "forbidden by God."

From a theoretical point of view, this conception has a number of pleasing features. It immediately solves the old problem about the subjectivity/objectivity of ethics. According to this theory, ethics is not merely a matter of personal feelings or social custom. Whether something is right or wrong is a perfectly objective matter: it is right if God commands it, wrong if God forbids it. Moreover, the Divine Command Theory suggests an answer to the perennial question of why anyone should bother with morality. Why not just look out for one's own interests? If immorality is the violation of God's commandments, there is an easy answer: on the day of final reckoning, you will be held accountable.

There are, however, serious problems for the theory. Of course, atheists would not accept it, because they do not believe that God exists. But the problems that arise are not merely problems for atheists. There are difficulties even for believers. The main problem was first noted by Plato, the Greek philosopher who lived 400 years before the birth of Jesus.

Plato's writings were in the form of dialogues, usually between Socrates and one or more interlocutors. In one of these dialogues, the *Euthyphro,* there is a discussion concerning whether "right" can be defined as "that which the gods command." Socrates is skeptical and asks: *Is conduct right because the gods command it, or do the gods command it because it is right?* It is one of the most famous questions in the history of philosophy. The contemporary British philosopher Antony Flew suggests that "one good test of a person's aptitude for philosophy is to discover whether he can grasp its force and point."

The point is this. If we accept the theological conception of right and wrong, we are caught in a dilemma. Socrates's question asks us to clarify what we mean. There are two things we might mean, and both options lead to trouble.

1. First, we might mean that conduct is right *because God commands it.* For example, according to Exodus 20:16, God commands us to be truthful. On this option, the *reason* we should be truthful is simply that God requires it. Apart from the divine command, truth telling is neither good nor bad. It is God's command that *makes* truthfulness right.

But this leads to trouble, for it represents God's commands as arbitrary. It means that God could have given *different* commands just as easily. He could have commanded us to be liars, and then lying, and not truthfulness, would be right. (You may be tempted to reply: "But God would never command us to be liars!" But why not? If he did endorse lying, God would not be commanding us to do wrong, because his command would make lying right.) Remember that on this view, honesty was not right *before* God commanded it. Therefore, he could have had no more reason to command it than its opposite; and so, from a moral point of view, his command is perfectly arbitrary.

Moreover, on this view, the doctrine of the goodness of God is reduced to nonsense. It is important to religious believers that God is not only all-powerful and all-knowing, but that he is also *good*; yet if we accept the idea that good and bad are defined by reference to God's will, this notion is deprived of any meaning. What could it mean to say that God's commands are good? If "X is good" simply means "X is commanded by God," then "God's commands are good" would mean only "God's commands are commanded by God"—an empty truism. In his *Discourse on Metaphysics* (1686) Leibniz put the point very clearly:

> So in saying that things are not good by any rule of goodness, but sheerly by the will of God, it seems to me that one destroys, without realizing it, all the love of God and all his glory. For why praise him for what he has done if he would be equally praiseworthy in doing exactly the contrary?

Thus if we choose the first of Socrates's two options, we are stuck with consequences that even the most religious people must find unacceptable.

2. There is a way to avoid these troublesome consequences. We can take the second of Socrates's options. We need not say that right conduct is right because God commands it. Instead, we may say that God commands right conduct *because it is right*. God, who is infinitely wise, realizes that truthfulness is far

better than deceitfulness, and so he commands us to be truthful; he sees that killing is wrong, and so he commands us not to kill; and so on for all the commandments.

If we take this option, we avoid the troublesome consequences that plagued the first alternative. God's commands turn out to be not at all arbitrary; they are the result of his wisdom in knowing what is best. And the doctrine of the goodness of God is preserved: to say that his commands are good means that he commands only what, in perfect wisdom, he sees to be the best. But this option leads to a different problem, which is equally troublesome for the theological conception of right and wrong: indeed, in taking this option, we have virtually *abandoned* the theological conception of right and wrong.

If we say that God commands us to be truthful because truthfulness is right, then we are admitting that there is some standard of right and wrong that is independent of God's will. We are saying that God *sees* or *recognizes* that truthfulness is right: this is very different from his *making* it right. The rightness exists prior to and independent of God's command, and it is the reason for the command. Thus if we want to know why we should be truthful, the reply "Because God commands it" will not take us very far. We may still ask "But why does God command it?" and the answer to *that* question will provide the underlying reasons why truthfulness is a good thing.

All this may be summarized in the following argument:

(1) Suppose God commands us to do what is right. Then *either* (a) the right actions are right because he commands them *or* (b) he commands them because they are right.

(2) If we take option (a), then God's commands are, from a moral point of view, arbitrary; moreover, the doctrine of the goodness of God is rendered meaningless.

(3) If we take option (b), then we have admitted there is

a standard of right and wrong that is independent of God's will.

(4) Therefore, we must *either* regard God's commands as arbitrary, and give up the doctrine of the goodness of God, *or* admit that there is a standard of right and wrong that is independent of his will, and give up the theological definitions of right and wrong.

(5) From a religious point of view, it is undesirable to regard God's commands as arbitrary or to give up the doctrine of the goodness of God.

(6) Therefore, even from a religious point of view, a standard of right and wrong that is independent of God's will must be accepted.

Many religious people believe that they should accept a theological conception of right and wrong because it would be impious not to do so. They feel, somehow, that if they believe in God, they *should* think that right and wrong are to be defined ultimately in terms of his will. But this argument suggests otherwise: it suggests that, on the contrary, the Divine Command Theory of right and wrong itself leads to impious results, so that a pious person should *not* accept it. And in fact, some of the greatest theologians, such as St. Thomas Aquinas (ca. 1225–1274), rejected the theory for just this reason.

TWO

IS GOD OMNIPOTENT?

Peter Geach

It is fortunate for my purposes that English has the two words "almighty" and "omnipotent," and that apart from any stipulation by me the words have rather different associations and suggestions. "Almighty" is the familiar word that comes in the creeds of the Church; "omnipotent" is at home rather in formal theological discussions and controversies, e.g., about miracles and about the problem of evil. . . . I shall use the word "almighty" to express God's power over all things, and I shall take "omnipotence" to mean ability to do everything.

I think we can in a measure understand what God's almightiness implies, and I shall argue that almightiness so understood must be ascribed to God if we are to retain anything like Christian belief in God. The position as regards omnipotence, or as regards the statement "God can do everything," seems to me to be very different. Of course even "God can do everything" may be understood simply as a way of magnifying God by contrast with the impotence of man. . . . I have no objection to such ways of speaking if they merely express a desire to give the best honour we can to God our Maker, whose Name only is excellent and whose praise is above heaven and earth. But theologians have tried *to prove* that God can do everything, or to derive conclusions from this thesis as a premise. I think such attempts have been wholly unsuccessful. When people have tried to read into "God can do everything" a signification not of Pious Intention but of Philosophical Truth, they have only landed themselves in intractable problems and hopeless confusions; no graspable sense has ever been given to this sentence that did not lead to self-contradiction or at least to conclusions manifestly untenable from a Christian point of view.

I shall return to this; but I must first develop what I have to say about God's almightiness, or power over all things. God is not just more powerful than any creature; no creature can compete with God in power, even unsuccessfully. For God is also the source of all power; any power a creature has comes from God and is maintained only for such time as God wills. Nebuchadnezzar submitted to praise and adore the God of heaven because he was forced by experience to realize that only by God's favour did his wits hold together from one end of a blasphemous sentence to the other end. Nobody can deceive God or circumvent him or frustrate him; and there is no question of God's trying to do anything and failing. In Heaven and on Earth, God does whatever he will. We shall see that some propositions of the form "God cannot do so-and-so" have to be accepted as true; but what God cannot be said to be able to do he likewise cannot will to do; we cannot drive a logical wedge between his power and his will, which are, as the Scholastics said, really identical, and there is no application to God of the concept of trying but failing.

I shall not spend time on citations of Scripture and tradition to show that this doctrine of God's almightiness is authentically Christian; nor shall I here develop rational grounds for believing it is a true doctrine. But it is quite easy to show that this doctrine is indispensable for Christianity, not a bit of old metaphysical luggage that can be abandoned with relief. For Christianity requires an absolute faith in the promises of God:

specifically, faith in the promise that some day the whole human race will be delivered and blessed by the establishment of the Kingdom of God. If God were not almighty, he might will and not do; sincerely promise, but find fulfilment beyond his power. Men might prove untamable and incorrigible, and might kill themselves through war or pollution before God's salvific plan for them could come into force. It is useless to say that after the end of this earthly life men would live again; for . . . only the promise of God can give us any confidence that there will be an afterlife for men, and if God were not almighty, this promise too might fail. If God is true and just and unchangeable and almighty, we can have absolute confidence in his promises: otherwise we cannot—and there would be an end of Christianity.

A Christian must therefore believe that God is almighty; but he need not believe that God can do everything. Indeed, the very argument I have just used shows that a Christian must not believe that God can do everything: for he may not believe that God could possibly break his own word. Nor can a Christian even believe that God can do everything that is logically possible; for breaking one's word is certainly a logically possible feat.

It seems to me, therefore, that the tangles in which people have enmeshed themselves when trying to give the expression "God can do everything" an intelligible and acceptable content are tangles that a Christian believer has no need to enmesh himself in; the spectacle of others enmeshed may sadden him, but need not cause him to stumble in the way of faith. The denial that God is omnipotent, or able to do everything, may seem dishonouring to God; but when we see where the contrary affirmation, in its various forms, has led, we may well cry out with Hobbes: "Can any man think God is served with such absurdities? . . . As if it were an acknowledgment of the Divine Power, to say, that which is, is not; or that which has been, has not been."

I shall consider four main theories of omnipotence. The first holds that God can do everything absolutely; everything that can be expressed in a string of words that makes sense; even if that sense can be shown to be self-contradictory, God is not bound in action, as we are in thought, by the laws of logic. I shall speak of this as the doctrine that God is *absolutely* omnipotent.

The second doctrine is that a proposition "God can do so-and-so" is true when and only when "so-and-so" represents a logically consistent description.

The third doctrine is that "God *can* do so-and-so" is true just if "God does so-and-so" is logically consistent. This is a weaker doctrine than the second; for "God is doing so-and-so" is logically consistent only when "so-and-so" represents a logically consistent description, but on the other hand there may be consistently describable feats which it would involve contradiction to suppose done *by God*.

The last and weakest view is that the realm of what can be done or brought about includes all future possibilities, and that whenever "God *will* bring so-and-so about" is logically possible, "God *can* bring so-and-so about" is true.

The first sense of "omnipotent" in which people have believed God to be omnipotent implies precisely: ability to do absolutely everything, everything describable. You mention it, and God can do it. . . . [A]t least one great philosopher, Descartes, deliberately adopted and defended this doctrine of omnipotence: what I shall call the doctrine of absolute omnipotence.

As Descartes himself remarked, nothing is too absurd for some philosopher to have said it some time; I once read an article about an Indian school of philosophers who were alleged to maintain that it is only a delusion, which the wise can overcome, that anything exists at all—so perhaps it would not matter all that much that a philosopher is found to defend absolute omnipotence. Perhaps it would not matter all that much that the philosopher in question was a very great one; for very great philosophers have maintained the most preposterous theses. What does make the denial of absolute omnipotence important is not that we are thereby denying what a philosopher, a very great philosopher, thought he must assert, but that this doctrine has a live influence on people's religious thought—I should of course say, a pernicious influence. Some naive Christians would explicitly assert the doctrine; and moreover, . . . a covert appeal to the doctrine is sometimes made even by people who would deny it if it were explicitly stated to them and its manifest consequences pointed out. . . .

For many years I used to teach the philosophy of Descartes in a special course for undergraduates reading French; year by year, there were always two or three of them who embraced Descartes's defence of absolute omnipotence *con amore* and protested indignantly when I described the doctrine as incoherent. It would of course have been no good to say I was following Doctors of the Church in rejecting the doctrine; I did in the end find a way of producing silence, though not, I fear, conviction, and going on to other topics of discussion; I cited the passages of the Epistle to the Hebrews which say explicitly that God cannot swear by anything greater than himself (vi. 13) or break his word (vi. 18). . . .

Let us leave these naive defenders in their entrenched position and return for a moment to Descartes. Descartes held that the truths of logic and arithmetic are freely made to be true by God's will. . . .

Descartes's motive for believing in absolute omnipotence was not contemptible: it seemed to him that otherwise God would be *subject* to the inexorable laws of logic as Jove was to the decrees of the Fates. The nature of logical truth is a very difficult problem, which I cannot discuss here. . . . But in the end I have to say that as we cannot say how a non-logical world would look, we cannot say how a supra-logical God would act or how he could communicate anything to us by way of revelation. So I end as I began: a Christian need not and cannot believe in absolute omnipotence.

It is important that Christians should clearly realize this, because otherwise a half-belief in absolute omnipotence may work in their minds subterraneously. . . . One and the same man may deny the doctrine of absolute omnipotence when the doctrine is clearly put to him, and yet reassure himself that God can certainly do so-and-so by using *merely* the premise of God's omnipotence. . . . At the very least this "so-and-so" must represent a logically consistent description of a feat; and proofs of logical consistency are notoriously not always easy. Nor, as we shall see, are our troubles at an end if we assume that God *can* do anything whose description is logically consistent.

Logical consistency in the description of the feat is certainly a *necessary* condition for the truth of "God can do so-and-so": if "so-and-so" represents an inconsistent description of a feat, then "God can do so-and-so" is certainly a false and impossible proposition. . . . And whereas only a minority of Christians have explicitly believed in absolute omnipotence, many have believed that a proposition of the form "God can do so-and-so" is true whenever "so-and-so" represents a description of a logically possible feat. This is our second doctrine of omnipotence. One classic statement of this comes in the *Summa Theologica* Ia q. xxv art. 3. Aquinas rightly says that we cannot explain "God can do everything" in terms of what is within the power of some agent; for "God can do everything any created agent can do," though true, is not a comprehensive enough account of God's power, which exceeds that of any created agent; and "God can do everything God can do" runs uselessly in a circle. So he puts forward the view that if the description "so-and-so" is in itself possible through the relation of the terms involved—if it does not involve contradictories' being true together—then "God can do so-and-so" is true. Many Christian writers have followed Aquinas in saying this;

but it is not a position consistently maintainable. As we shall see, Aquinas did not manage to stick to the position himself. . . . [T]here is nothing easier than to mention feats which are logically possible but which God cannot do, if Christianity is true. Lying and promise-breaking are logically possible feats: but Christian faith, as I have said, collapses unless we are assured that God cannot lie and cannot break his promises.

This argument is an *ad hominem* argument addressed to Christians; but there are well-known logical arguments to show that on any view there must be some logically possible feats that are beyond God's power. One good example suffices: making a thing which its maker cannot afterwards destroy. This is certainly a possible feat, a feat that some human beings have performed. Can God perform the feat or not? If he cannot there is already some logically possible feat which God cannot perform. If God can perform the feat, then let us suppose that he does. . . . Then we are supposing God to have brought about a situation in which he *has* made something he cannot destroy; and in that situation destroying this thing is a *logically* possible feat that God cannot accomplish, for we surely cannot admit the idea of a creature whose destruction is logically *impossible*. . . . So this notion of omnipotence, like the Cartesian idea of absolute omnipotence, turns out to be obviously incompatible with Christian faith, and moreover logically untenable.

Let us see, then, if we fare any better with the third theory: the theory that the only condition for the truth of "God can do so-and-so" is that "God does so-and-so" or "God is doing so-and-so" must be logically possible. As I said, this imposes a more restrictive condition than the second theory: for there are many feats that we can consistently suppose to be performed but cannot consistently suppose to be performed by God. This theory might thus get us out of the logical trouble that arose with the second theory about the feat: *making a thing that its maker cannot destroy*. For though this is a logically possible feat, a feat some creatures do perform, it might well be argued that "*God* has made a thing that its maker cannot destroy" is a proposition with a buried inconsistency in it; and if so, then on the present account of omnipotence we need not say "God *can* make a thing that its maker cannot destroy."

This suggestion also, however, can easily be refuted by an example of great philosophical importance that I borrow from Aquinas. "It comes about that Miss X never loses her virginity" is plainly a logically possible proposition: and so also is "God brings it about that Miss X never loses her virginity." All the same, if it so happens that Miss X already has lost her virginity, "God *can* bring it about that Miss X never loses her virginity" is false (Ia q. xxv art. 4). Before Miss X had lost her virginity, it would have been true to say this very thing; so what we can truly say about what God can do will be different at different times. This appears to imply a change in God, but Aquinas would certainly say, and I think rightly, that it doesn't really do so. It is just like the case of Socrates coming to be shorter than Theaetetus because Theaetetus grows up; here, the change is on the side of Theaetetus not of Socrates. So in our case, the change is really in Miss X not in God; something about her passes from the realm of possibility to the realm of *fait accompli*, and thus *no longer* comes under the concept of the accomplishable. . . . I think Aquinas's position here is strongly defensible; but if he does defend it, he has abandoned the position that God can do everything that it is not a priori impossible *for God to do*, let alone the position that God can bring about everything describable in a logically consistent way. . . .

Let us then consider our fourth try. Could it be said that the "everything" in "God can do everything" refers precisely to things that are not in the realm of *fait accompli* but of futurity? This will not do either. If God can promulgate promises to men, then as regards any promises that are not yet fulfilled we know that they certainly will be fulfilled: and in that case

God clearly has not a . . . two-way power of either actualizing the event that will fulfil the promise or not actualizing it. God can then only do what will fulfil his promise. And if we try to evade this by denying that God can make promises known to men, then we have once more denied something essential to Christian faith, and we are still left with something that God cannot do. . . .

Thus all the four theories of omnipotence that I have considered break down. Only the first overtly flouts logic; but the other three all involve logical contradictions, or so it seems; and moreover, all these theories have consequences fatal to the truth of Christian faith. The last point really ought not to surprise us; for the absolute confidence a Christian must have in God's revelation and promises involves, as I said at the outset, both a belief that God is almighty, in the sense I explained, and a belief that there are certain describable things that God cannot do and therefore will not do.

THREE

WHY DOES GOD ALLOW EVIL?

Richard Swinburne

The world . . . contains much evil. An omnipotent God could have prevented this evil, and surely a perfectly good and omnipotent God would have done so. So why is there this evil? Is not its existence strong evidence against the existence of God? It would be unless we can construct what is known as a theodicy, an explanation of why God would allow such evil to occur. I believe that that can be done, and I shall outline a theodicy. . . . I emphasize that . . . in writing that God would do this or that, I am not taking for granted the existence of God, but merely claiming that, if there is a God, it is to be expected that he would do certain things, including allowing the occurrence of certain evils; and so, I am claiming, their occurrence is not evidence against his existence.

It is inevitable that any attempt by myself or anyone else to construct a theodicy will sound callous, indeed totally insensitive to human suffering. Many theists, as well as atheists, have felt that any attempt to construct a theodicy evinces an immoral approach to suffering. I can only ask the reader to believe that I am not totally insensitive to human suffering, and that I do mind about the agony of poisoning, child abuse, bereavement, solitary imprisonment, and martial infidelity as much as anyone else. True, I would not in most cases recommend that a pastor give this chapter to victims of sudden distress at their worst moment to read for consolation. But this is not because its arguments are unsound; it is simply that most people in deep distress need comfort, not argument. Yet there is a problem about why God allows evil, and, if the theist does not have (in a cool moment) a satisfactory answer to it, then his belief in God is less than rational, and there is no reason why the atheist should share it. To appreciate the argument of this chapter, each of us needs to stand back a bit from the particular situation of his or her own life and that of close relatives and friends (which can so easily seem the only important thing in the world), and ask very generally what good things would a generous and everlasting God give to human beings in the course of a short earthly life. Of course thrills of pleasure and periods of contentment are good things, and—other things being equal—God would certainly seek to provide plenty of those. But a generous God will seek to give deeper good things than these. He will seek to give us great responsibility for ourselves, each other, and the world, and thus a share in his own creative activity of determining what sort of world it is to be. And he will seek to make our lives valuable, of great use to ourselves and each other. The problem is that God cannot give us these goods in full measure without allowing much evil on the way. . . .

[T]here are plenty of evils, positive bad states, which God could if he chose remove. I divide these into moral evils and natural evils. I understand by "natural evil" all evil which is not deliberately produced by human beings and which is not allowed by human beings to occur as a result of their negligence. Natural evil includes both physical suffering and mental suffering, of animals as well as humans; all the trial of suffering which disease, natural disasters, and accidents unpredictable by humans bring in their train. "Moral evil" I understand as including all evil caused deliberately by humans doing what they ought not to do (or allowed to occur by humans negligently failing to do what they ought to do) *and* also the evil constituted by such deliberate actions or negligent failure. It includes the sensory pain of the blow inflicted by the bad parent on his child, the mental pain of the parent depriving the child of love, the starvation allowed to occur in Africa because of negligence by members of foreign governments who could have prevented it, and also the evil of the parent or politician deliberately bringing about the pain or not trying to prevent the starvation.

Moral Evil

The central core of any theodicy must, I believe, be the "free-will defence," which deals—to start with—with moral evil, but can be extended to deal with much natural evil as well. The free-will defence claims that it is a great good that humans have certain sort of free will which I shall call free and responsible choice, but that, if they do, then necessarily there will be the natural possibility of moral evil. (By the "natural possibility" I mean that it will not be determined in advance whether or not the evil will occur.) A God who gives humans such free will necessarily brings about the possibility, and puts outside his own control whether or not that evil occurs. It is not logically possible—that is, it would be self-contradictory to suppose—that God could give us such free will and yet ensure that we always use it in the right way.

Free and responsible choice is not just free will in the narrow sense of being able to choose between alternative actions, without our choice being causally necessitated by some prior cause. . . . [H]umans could have that kind of free will merely in virtue of being able to choose freely between two equally good and unimportant alternatives. Free and responsible choice is rather free will (of the kind discussed) to make significant choices between good and evil, which make a big difference to the agent, to others, and to the world.

Given that we have free will, we certainly have free and responsible choice. Let us remind ourselves of the difference that humans can make to themselves, others, and the world. Humans have opportunities to give themselves and others pleasurable sensations, and to pursue worthwhile activities—to play tennis or the piano, to acquire knowledge of history and science and philosophy, and to help others to do so, and thereby to build deep personal relations founded upon such sensations and activities. And humans are so made that they can form their characters. Aristotle famously remarked: "we become just by doing just acts, prudent by doing prudent acts, brave by doing brave acts." That is, by doing a just act when it is difficult—when it goes against our natural inclinations (which is what I understand by desires)—we make it easier to do a just act next time. We can gradually change our desires, so that—for example—doing just acts becomes natural. Thereby we can free ourselves from the power of the less good desires to which we are subject. And, by choosing to acquire knowledge and to use it to build machines of various sorts, humans can extend the range of the differences they can make to the world—they can build universities to last for centuries, or save energy for the next generation; and by cooperative effort over many decades they can eliminate poverty. The possibilities for free and responsible choice are enormous.

It is good that the free choices of humans should include *genuine* responsibility for other humans, and that involves the opportunity to benefit *or* harm them. God has the power to benefit or to harm humans. If other agents are to be given a share in his creative work, it is good that they have that power too (although perhaps to a lesser degree). A world in which agents can benefit each other but not do each other harm is one where they have only very limited responsibility for each other. If my responsibility for you is limited to whether or not to give you a camcorder, but I cannot cause you pain, stunt your growth, or limit your education, then I do not have a great deal of responsibility for you. A God who gave agents only such limited responsibilities for their fellows would not have given much. God would have reserved for himself the all-important choice of the kind of world it was to be, while simply allowing humans the minor choice of filling in the details. He would be like a father asking his elder son to look after the younger son, and adding that he would be watching the elder son's every move and would intervene the moment the elder son did a thing wrong. The elder son might justly retort that, while he would be happy to share his father's work, he could really do so only if he were left to make his own judgements as to what to do within a significant range of the options available to the father. A good God, like a good father, will delegate responsibility. In order to allow creatures a share in creation, he will allow them the choice of hurting and maiming, of frustrating the divine plan. Our world is one where creatures have just such deep responsibility for each other. I cannot only benefit my children, but harm them. One way in which I can harm them is that I can inflict physical pain on them. But there are much more damaging things which I can do to them. Above all I can stop them growing into creatures with significant knowledge, power, and freedom; I can determine whether they come to have the kind of free and responsible choice which I have. The possibility of humans bringing about significant evil is a logical consequence of their having this free and responsible choice. Not even God could give us this choice without the possibility of resulting evil.

Now . . . an action would not be intentional unless it was done for a reason—that is, seen as in some way a good thing (either in itself or because of its consequences). And, if reasons alone influence actions, that regarded by the subject as most important will determine what is done; an agent under the influence of reason alone will inevitably do the action which he regards as overall the best. If an agent does not do the action which he regards as overall the best, he must have allowed factors other than reason to exert an influence on him. In other words, he must have allowed desires for what he regards as good only in a certain respect, but not overall, to influence his conduct. So, in order to have a choice between good and evil, agents need already a certain depravity, in the sense of a system of desires for what they correctly believe to be evil. I need to *want* to overeat, get more than my fair share of money or power, indulge my sexual appetites even by deceiving my spouse or partner, want to see you hurt, if I am to have choice between good and evil. This depravity is itself an evil which is a necessary condition of a greater good. It makes possible a choice made seriously and deliberately, because made in the face of a genuine alternative. I stress that, according to the free-will defence, it is the natural possibility of moral evil which is the necessary condition of the great good, not the actual evil itself. Whether that occurs is (through God's choice) outside God's control and up to us.

Note further and crucially that, if I suffer in consequence of your freely chosen bad action, that is not by any means pure loss for me. In a certain respect it is good for *me*. My suffering would be pure loss for me if the only good thing in life was sensory pleasure, and the only bad thing sensory pain; and it is because the modern world tends to think in those terms that the problem of evil seems so acute. If these were the only good and bad things, the occurrence of suffering would indeed be a conclusive objection to the existence of God. But we have already noted the great good of freely choosing and influencing our future, that of our fellows, and that of the world. And now note another great good—the good of our life serving a purpose, of being of use to ourselves and others. Recall the words of Christ, "it is more blessed to give than to receive" (as quoted by St. Paul [Acts 20:35]). We tend to think, when the beggar appears on our doorstep and we feel obliged to give and do give, that that was lucky for him but not for us who happened to be at home. That is not what Christ's words say. They say that *we* are the lucky ones, not just because we have a lot, out of which we can give a little, but because we are privileged to contribute to the beggar's happiness—and that privilege is worth a lot more than money. And, just as it is a great good freely to choose to do good, so it is also a good to be used by someone else for a worthy purpose (so long, that is, that he or she has the right, the authority, to use us in this way). Being allowed to suffer to make possible a great good is a privilege, even if the privilege is forced upon you. Those who are allowed to die for their country and thereby save their country from foreign oppression are privileged. Cultures less obsessed than our own by the evil of purely physical pain have always recognized that. And they have recognized that it is still a blessing, even if the one who died had been conscripted to fight.

And even twentieth-century man can begin to see that— sometimes—when he seeks to help prisoners, not by giving them more comfortable quarters, but by letting them help the handicapped; or when he pities rather than envies the "poor little rich girl" who has everything and does nothing for anyone else. And one phenomenon prevalent in end-of-century Britain draws this especially to our attention—the evil of unemployment. Because of our system of Social Security, the unemployed on the whole have enough money to live without too much discomfort; certainly they are a lot better off than are many employed in Africa or Asia or Victorian Britain. What is evil about unemployment is not so much any resulting poverty but the uselessness of the unemployed. They often report feeling unvalued by society, of no use, "on the scrap heap." They rightly think it would be a good for them to contribute; but they cannot. Many of them would welcome a system where they were obliged to do useful work in preference to one where society has no use for them.

It follows from that fact that being of use is a benefit for him who is of use, and that those who suffer at the hands of others, and thereby make possible the good of those others who have free and responsible choice, are themselves benefited in this respect. I am fortunate if the natural possibility of my suffering if you choose to hurt me is the vehicle which makes your choice really matter. My vulnerability, my openness to suffering (which necessarily involves my actually suffering if you make the wrong choice), means that you are not just like a pilot in a simulator, where it does not matter if mistakes are made. That our choices matter tremendously, that we can make great differences to things for good or ill, is one of the greatest gifts a creator can give us. And if my suffering is the means by which he can give you that choice, I too am in this respect fortunate. Though of course suffering is in itself a bad thing, my good fortune is that the suffering is not random, pointless suffering. It is suffering which is a consequence of my vulnerability which makes me of such use.

Someone may object that the only good thing is not *being* of use (dying for one's country or being vulnerable to suffering at your hands), but *believing* that one is of use—believing that one is dying for one's country and that this is of use; the "feel-good" experience. But that cannot be correct. Having comforting beliefs is only a good thing if they are true beliefs. It is not a good thing to believe that things are going well when they are not, or that your life is of use when it is not. Getting pleasure out of comforting falsehood is a cheat. But if I get pleasure out of a true belief, it must be that I regard the state of things which I believe to hold to be a good thing. If I get pleasure out of the true belief that my daughter is doing well at school, it must be that I regard it as a good thing that my daughter does well at school (whether or not I believe that she is doing well). If I did not think the latter, I would not get any pleasure out of believing that she is doing well. Likewise, the belief that I am vulnerable to suffering at your hands, and that that is a good thing, can only be a good thing if being vulnerable to suffering at your hands is itself a good thing (independently of whether I believe it or not). Certainly, when my life is of use and that is a good for me, it is even better if I believe it and get comfort therefrom; but it can only be even better if it is already a good for me whether I believe it or not.

But though suffering may in these ways serve good purposes, does God have the right to allow me to suffer for your benefit, without asking my permission? For surely, an objector will say, no one has the right to allow one person A to suffer for the benefit of another one B without A's consent. We judge that doctors who use patients as involuntary objects of experimentation in medical experiments which they hope will produce results which can be used to benefit others are doing something wrong. After all, if my arguments about the utility of suffering are sound, ought we not all to be causing suffering to others in order that those others may have the opportunity to react in the right way?

There are, however, crucial differences between God and the doctors. The first is that God as the author of our being has certain rights, a certain authority over us, which we do not have over our fellow humans. He is the cause of our existence at each moment of our existence and sustains the laws of nature which give us everything we are and have. To allow someone to suffer for his own good or that of others, one has to stand in some kind of parental relationship towards him. I do not have the right to let some stranger suffer for the sake of some good, when I could easily prevent this, but I do have *some* right of his kind in respect of my own children. I may let the younger son suffer *somewhat* for his own good or that of his brother. I have this right because in small part I am responsible for the younger son's existence, his beginning and continuance. If I have begotten him, nourished, and educated him, I have some limited rights over him in return; to a *very limited* extent I can use him for some worthy purpose. If this is correct, then a God who is so much more the author of our being than are our parents has so much more right in this respect. Doctors do not have over us even the rights of parents.

But secondly and all-importantly, the doctors *could* have asked the patients for permission; and the patients, being free agents of some power and knowledge, could have made an informed choice of whether or not to allow themselves to be used. By contrast, God's choice is not about how to use already existing agents, but about the sort of agents to make and the sort of world into which to put them. In God's situation there are no agents to be asked. I am arguing that it is good that one agent A should have deep responsibility for another B (who in turn could have deep responsibility for another C). It is not logically possible for God to have asked B if he wanted things thus, for, if A is to be responsible for B's growth in freedom, knowledge, and power, there will not be a B with enough freedom and knowledge to make any choice, before God has to choose whether or not to give A responsibility for him. One cannot ask a baby into which sort of world he or she wishes to be born. The creator has to make the choice independently of his creatures. He will seek on balance to benefit them—all of them. And, in giving them the gift of life— whatever suffering goes with it—that is a substantial benefit. But when one suffers at the hands of another, often perhaps it is not enough of a benefit to outweigh the suffering. Here is the point to recall that it is an additional benefit to the sufferer that his suffering is the means whereby the one who hurt him had the opportunity to make a significant choice between good and evil which otherwise he would not have had.

Although for these reasons, as I have been urging, God has the right to allow humans to cause each other to suffer, there must be a limit to the amount of suffering which he has the right to allow a human being to suffer for the sake of a great good. A parent may allow an elder child to have the power to do some harm to a younger child for the sake of the responsibility given to the elder child; but there are limits. And there are limits even to the moral right of God, our creator and sustainer, to use free sentient beings as pawns in a greater game. Yet, if these limits were too narrow, God would be unable to give humans much real responsibility; he would be able to allow them only to play a toy game. Still, limits there must be to God's rights to allow humans to hurt each other; and limits there are in the world to the extent to which they can hurt each other, provided above all by the short finite life enjoyed by humans and other creatures—one human can hurt another for no more than eighty years or so. And there are a number of other safety-devices in-built into our physiology and psychology, limiting the amount of pain we can suffer. But the primary safety limit is that provided by the shortness of our finite life. Unending, unchosen suffering would indeed to my mind provide a very strong argument against the existence of God. But that is not the human situation.

So then God, without asking humans, has to choose for them between the kinds of world in which they can live—basically either a world in which there is very little opportunity for humans to benefit or harm each other, or a world in which there is considerable opportunity. How shall he choose? There are clearly reasons for both choices. But it seems to me (just, on balance) that his choosing to create the world in which we have considerable opportunity to benefit or harm each other is to bring about a good at least as great as the evil which he thereby allows to occur. *Of course* the suffering he allows is a bad thing; and, other things being equal, to be avoided. But having the natural possibility of causing suffering makes possible a greater good. God, in creating humans who (of logical necessity) cannot choose for themselves the kind of world into which they are to come, plausibly exhibits his goodness in making for them the heroic choice that they come into a risky world where they may have to suffer for the good of others.

Natural Evil

Natural evil is not to be accounted for along the same lines as moral evil. Its main role rather, I suggest, is to make it possible for humans to have the kind of choice which the free-will defence extols, and to make available to humans specially worthwhile kinds of choice.

There are two ways in which natural evil operates to give humans those choices. First, the operation of natural laws producing evils gives humans knowledge (if they choose to seek it) of how to bring about such evils themselves. Observing you catch some disease by the operation of natural processes gives me the power either to use those processes to give that disease to other people, or through negligence to allow others to catch it, or to take measures to prevent others from catching the disease. Study of the mechanisms of nature producing various evils (and goods) opens up for humans a wide range of choice. This is the way in which in fact we learn how to bring about (good and) evil. But could not God give us the requisite knowledge (of how to bring about good or evil) which we need in order to have free and responsible choice by a less costly means? Could he not just whisper in our ears from time to time what are the different consequences of different actions of ours? Yes. But anyone who believed that an action of his would have some effect because he believed that God had told him so would see all his actions as done under the all-watchful eye of God. He would not merely believe strongly that there was a God, but would know it with real certainty. That knowledge would greatly inhibit his freedom of choice, would make it very difficult for him to choose to do evil. This is because we all have a natural inclination to wish to be thought well of by everyone, and above all by an all-good God; that we have such an inclination is a very good feature of humans, without which we would be less than human. Also, if we were directly informed of the consequences of our actions, we would be deprived of the choice whether to seek to discover what the consequences were through experiment and hard cooperative work. Knowledge would be available on tap. Natural processes alone give humans knowledge of the effects of their actions without inhibiting their freedom, and if evil is to be a possibility for them they must know how to allow it to occur.

The other way in which natural evil operates to give humans their freedom is that it makes possible certain kinds of action towards it between which agents can choose. It increases the range of significant choice. A particular natural evil, such as a physical pain, gives to the sufferer a choice—whether to endure it with patience, or to bemoan his lot. His friend can choose whether to show compassion towards the sufferer, or to be callous. The pain makes possible these choices, which would not otherwise exist. There is no guarantee that our actions in response to the pain will be good ones, but the pain gives us the opportunity to perform good actions. The good or bad actions which we perform in the face of natural evil themselves provide opportunities for further choice—of good or evil stances towards the former actions. If I am patient with my suffering, you can choose whether to encourage or laugh at my patience; if I bemoan my lot, you can teach me by word and example what a good thing patience is. If you are sympathetic, I have then the opportunity to show gratitude for the sympathy; or to be so self-involved that I ignore it. If you are callous, I can choose whether to ignore this or to resent it for life. And so on. I do not think that there can be much doubt that natural evil, such as physical pain, makes available these sorts of choice. The actions which natural evil makes possible are ones which allow us to perform at our best and interact with our fellows at the deepest level.

It may, however, be suggested that adequate opportunity for these great good actions would be provided by the occurrence of moral evil without any need for suffering to be caused by

natural processes. You can show courage when threatened by a
gunman, as well as when threatened by cancer; and show sympathy to those likely to be killed by gunmen as well as to
those likely to die of cancer. But just imagine all the suffering
of mind and body caused by disease, earthquake, and accident
unpreventable by humans removed at a stroke from our society. No sickness, no bereavement in consequence of the un-
timely death of the young. Many of us would then have such
an easy life that we simply would not have much opportunity
to show courage or, indeed, manifest much in the way of great
goodness at all. We need those insidious processes of decay and
dissolution which money and strength cannot ward off for
long to give us the opportunities, so easy otherwise to avoid,
to become heroes.

God has the right to allow natural evils to occur (for the
same reason as he has the right to allow moral evils to occur)—up to a limit. It would, of course, be crazy for God to
multiply evils more and more in order to give endless opportunity for heroism, but to have *some* significant opportunity for
real heroism and consequent character formation is a benefit
for the person to whom it is given. Natural evils give to us the
knowledge to make a range of choices between good and evil,
and the opportunity to perform actions of especially valuable
kinds.

There is, however, no reason to suppose that animals have
free will. So what about their suffering? Animals had been suffering for a long time before humans appeared on this
planet—just how long depends on which animals are conscious beings. The first thing to take into account here is that,
while the higher animals, at any rate the vertebrates, suffer, it is
most unlikely that they suffer nearly as much as humans do.
Given that suffering depends directly on brain events (in turn
caused by events in other parts of the body), then, since the
lower animals do not suffer at all and humans suffer a lot, animals of intermediate complexity (it is reasonable to suppose)

suffer only a moderate amount. So, while one does need a theodicy to account for why God allows animals to suffer, one does not need as powerful a theodicy as one does in respect of humans. One only needs reasons adequate to account for God allowing an amount of suffering much less than that of humans. That said, there is, I believe, available for animals parts of the theodicy which I have outlined above for humans.

The good of animals, like that of humans, does not consist solely in thrills of pleasure. For animals, too, there are more worthwhile things, and in particular intentional actions, and among them serious significant intentional actions. The life of animals involves many serious significant intentional actions. Animals look for a mate, despite being tired and failing to find one. They take great trouble to build nests and feed their young, to decoy predators and explore. But all this inevitably involves pain (going on despite being tired) and danger. An animal cannot intentionally avoid forest fires, or take trouble to rescue its offspring from forest fires, unless there exists a serious danger of getting caught in a forest fire. The action of rescuing despite danger simply cannot be done unless the danger exists—and the danger will not exist unless there is a significant natural probability of being caught in the fire. Animals do not choose freely to do such actions, but the actions are nevertheless worthwhile. It is great that animals feed their young, not just themselves; that animals explore when they know it to be dangerous; that animals save each other from predators, and so on. These are the things that give the lives of animals their value. But they do often involve some suffering to some creature.

To return to the central case of humans—the reader will agree with me to the extent to which he or she values responsibility, free choice, and being of use very much more than thrills of pleasure or absence of pain. There is no other way to get the evils of this world into the right perspective, except to reflect at length on innumerable very detailed thought experiments (in addition to actual experiences of life) in which we postulate very different sorts of worlds from our own, and then ask ourselves whether the perfect goodness of God would require him to create one of these (or no world at all) rather than our own. But I conclude with a very small thought experiment, which may help to begin this process. Suppose that you exist in another world before your birth in this one, and are given a choice as to the sort of life you are to have in this one. You are told that you are to have only a short life, maybe of only a few minutes, although it will be an adult life in the sense that you will have the richness of sensation and belief characteristic of adults. You have a choice as to the sort of life you will have. You can have either a few minutes of very considerable pleasure, of the kind produced by some drug such as heroin, which you will experience by yourself and which will have no effects at all in the world (for example, no one else will know about it); or you can have a few minutes of considerable pain, such as the pain of childbirth, which will have (unknown to you at the time of pain) considerable good effects on others over a few years. You are told that, if you do not make the second choice, those others will never exist—and so you are under no moral obligation to make the second choice. But you seek to make the choice which will make *your* own life the best life for *you* to have led. How will you choose? The choice is, I hope, obvious. You should choose the second alternative.

For someone who remains unconvinced by my claims about the relative strengths of the good and evils involved—holding that, great though the goods are, they do not justify the evils which they involve—there is a fallback position. My arguments may have convinced you of the greatness of the goods involved sufficiently for you to allow that a perfectly good God would be justified in bringing about the evils for the sake of the good which they make possible, if and only if God also provided compensation in the form of happiness after death to the victims whose sufferings make possible the good. . . . While believing that God does provide at any rate for many humans such life after death, I have expounded a theodicy without relying on this assumption. But I can understand someone thinking that the assumption is needed, especially when we are considering the worst evils. (This compensatory afterlife need not necessarily be the everlasting life of Heaven.)

It remains the case, however, that evil is evil, and there is a substantial price to pay for the goods of our world which it makes possible. God would not be less than perfectly good if he created instead a world without pain and suffering, and so without the particular goods which those evils make possible. Christian, Islamic, and much Jewish tradition claims that God has created worlds of both kinds—our world, and the Heaven of the blessed. The latter is a marvelous world with a vast range of possible deep goods, but it lacks a few goods which our world contains, including the good of being able to reject the good. A generous God might well choose to give some of us the choice of rejecting the good in a world like ours before giving to those who embrace it a wonderful world in which the former possibility no longer exists.

FOUR

IS GOD OBLIGED TO MAKE US HAPPY?

George N. Schlesinger

I

The world is full of suffering. God is either helpless to prevent it, in which case He is not all-powerful, or does not choose to prevent it, in which case He is not all-good. For generations this has been regarded as the most effective argument against the belief that an omnipotent and omnibenevolent being exists. Naturally, theists have tried their hardest to come up with an adequate reply.

Among the numerous suggestions as to how to meet the atheistic challenge we find some that contain important religious ideas yet, unfortunately, do not mitigate the problem. Many of us have heard it said that (1) we must not take for granted all the joy and moral beauty in the world, which by far outstrips the amount of existing pain and moral ugliness; or that (2) all suffering ultimately brings about a greater good and hence is not to be regarded as evil.

There is wisdom in these sayings, but they are irrelevant to the problem of evil. Multiply or divide the amount of pain in the world by a billion, and its incompatibility with divine goodness and omnipotence is not affected. If even a single individual had to endure unnecessarily a slight inconvenience for a brief moment, the problem, although it would not hurt so much or possibly not even be noticed by anyone, would be logically just as real.[1] And without wishing to deny the truth of point (2) or its optimistic implication, it cannot contribute anything to the solution of our problem. For we may ask: why did God in His omnipotence not create for us all the benefits referred to in (2) without our having to pay for them first in pain?

Another suggestion, no longer very much discussed, is that suffering is always chastisement for transgressions and hence is well-deserved and does not amount to evil. One of the objections a sceptic may raise against this is: why have opportunities to sin been created? In an attempt to defend himself, the theist might wish to claim that human free will is very precious and that we cannot have it unless people are free to sin. This attempt can be defeated by pointing out that it would be possible to have a world in which there are free agents but no one is punished, for God could have created free agents who He knows prior to their birth will freely refrain from sinning.

Let me very briefly point out that one of the most discussed problems in the philosophy of religion . . . has been whether such a world is possible. Some very elaborate arguments have been advanced to show that it is logically impossible for God to create free agents who He can be certain will not sin. These prolonged debates provide striking illustration of the fascination that complex arguments may hold for some philosophers, who debate them with such zest that it never even occurs to them to pause and ask themselves: is there any point to these arguments? Indeed, it seems quite evident that they have no point at all. Suppose we ask: why did we have to have monsters like Hitler or Stalin? The theist would answer, according to the line of thought just reviewed, that God would not have prevented their coming into being unless He had made sure that there were no free agents at all. The creation of free agents inevitably carries the risk of some very wicked people being born.

But the atheist need not trouble himself to examine the soundness of the various arguments leading to this conclusion, since it is in any case of no help to the theist. He can readily grant that since the existence of free agents is an indispensable part of the Divine scheme of things, the birth of some vicious people is unavoidable. Still, a competent psychologist could have determined while Hitler was still an adolescent that he had a nefarious character and would be likely, if given the opportunity, to inflict much pain on others. It is reasonable to maintain that God could do this even earlier. Why then did a benevolent God not liquidate him or render him harmless by any other means at His disposal as soon as the wicked nature of Hitler became evident?

It may also be mentioned that the claim that all suffering is punishment for sins runs into another difficulty, since it cannot account for the suffering of innocent babies.

II

In order to gain real insight into the nature of Divine benevolence, we have to start from the beginning and ask: is there indeed evil in the world? Suffering unquestionably exists, but can this be construed as the existence of evil? Before one can answer this question one must assess the the moral status of divine acts. It is generally agreed that divine acts are assessed by the same criterion as human acts; otherwise the notions of "good" and "bad" would not retain their normal meanings. What then are evil human acts? As a rule they are acts which contravene moral obligations. This brings us to the question which must be answered first: what are my obligations toward my fellow man? On the surface, it may seem that my obligation toward another is to make him as happy as I can, provided this does not interfere with the welfare of others. Upon reflection, however, this appears inadequate.

Suppose I have under my care a child of very low intelligence but of very happy disposition. Provided his basic bodily needs are minimally taken care of, he enjoys lying on his back all day long and staring into the air. A minor operation, I am assured by the best medical authorities, would spectacularly raise his intelligence and render him capable of creative achievements as well as the appreciation of music, art, literature, and science. Naturally, if his intelligence were raised he would be vulnerable to the frustrations, disappointments, and anxieties most of us are subject to from time to time. Nevertheless, I believe it will be agreed that I should be reprehensible if I refrained from letting the child have the operation, even if I insured to the best of my ability that his physical needs would always be taken care of.

But why is it not good enough that I am keeping him in a state of maximum happiness? Apparently, the degree of desirability of a state is not a simple function of a single factor— namely, the degree to which one's wants are satisfied—but is also dependent on the kind of being one is. The somewhat less happy but intelligent child is ultimately better off than the happy idiot because, although the amount of happiness is less in his case, he is more than compensated for this by having become a preferable kind of person.

Thus, my moral obligations do not consist simply in having to endeavor to raise the amount of happiness a certain being is granted to enjoy. These obligations are somewhat more complex and consist in my having to raise the degree of desirability of his state, a two-valued function depending both on the potentials of the individual and the extent to which his needs are being taken care of. The idea may be illustrated as follows. In recent years much has been heard about machines that electrically stimulate the pleasure centers of one's brain.

Once a person's brain is connected to the machine, he becomes completely captivated by the experience it provides and desires absolutely nothing but the passive enjoyment of the sublime pleasures it induces. But I believe that most would condemn me if, without prior consultation, I hooked up A, a normal person, to this machine and thus caused him to become addicted to it for the rest of his life. This would be so even if I provided an attendant to look after A's vital physical needs. I should, I believe, be severely condemned, even though A's addiction has no ill after-effects. But A, previously a normal person, has had his usual ups and downs, while now he is in a continual state of "bliss." Shouldn't I be praised for having eliminated the large gap between his potential and actual amounts of happiness by having satiated him with pleasure?

The answer, I believe, is no, and not merely because I have rendered A a less useful member of society. Even if the needs of others are not taken into account, it will be agreed by most that by inducing in A a permanent state of euphoria I have not done a good thing to him. This is so because I have reduced the desirability of A's state. The latter is not solely a function of how satiated A is with pleasure but also of the kind of being he is. A was, prior to my interference, capable of a great variety of response, of interaction with others, of creativity and self-improvement, while now he is reduced to a completely inactive, vegetable-like existence. The great increase in the factor of happiness is insufficient to make up for the great loss in the second factor, A's being lowered from the state of a normal human being to the state of an inferior quasi-hibernating inert existence.

The general ethical view I am trying to explain, and which is quite widely accepted, is well-reflected in the famous dictum, "Better Socrates dissatisfied than the fool satisfied; better the fool dissatisfied than the pig satisfied." It suggests that given two different creatures A and B, with different capacities and appetites and different potentials for suffering and happiness, it may turn out that although A is satisfied with his lot while B is complaining, B is in a more desirable state than A. Accordingly, one of the universal rules of ethics is not, "if everything else is equal increase the state of happiness of A," but rather, "if everything is equal increase the degree of desirability of the state of A by as much as possible." It may be pointed out that generally I have far more opportunities to affect A's happiness than to affect the other factor which determines the degree of desirability of his state. It should also be noted that it is by no means always clear how much increase in one factor makes up for a given decrease in the other factor.

Now I take it that conceptually there is no limit to the degree which the desirability of state may reach. One can easily conceive a super-Socrates who has a much higher intelligence and many more than five senses through which to enjoy the world and who stands to Socrates as the latter stands to the pig. And there is the possibility of a super-super-Socrates and so on *ad infinitum*. Given this last supposition about an infinite hierarchy of possible beings and hence the limitlessness of the possible increase in the degree of desirability of state, how does the aforementioned universal ethical rule, ". . . increase the degree of desirability of state as much as possible," apply to God? After all, no matter to what degree it is increased it is always logically possible to increase it further. A mortal's possibilities are physically limited, hence in his case there is a natural limit to the principle; but there is no limit to what God can do. It is therefore logically impossible for Him to fulfill the ethical principle, i.e., to do enough to discharge His obligation to do more and further increase the degree of desirability of state. But what is logically impossible to do cannot be done by an omnipotent being either, and it is agreed by practically all philosophers that God's inability to do what is logically impossible does not diminish His omnipotence. Just as it is logically impossible to name the highest integer, it is impossible to grant a creature a degree of desirability of state higher than which in inconceivable; thus it is logically impossible for God to fulfill what is required by the universal ethical principle, and therefore He cannot fulfill it, and so is not obliged to fulfill it. There is no room for complaint, seeing that God has not fulfilled the ethical principle which mortals are bound by and has left His creatures in various low states of desirability. Thus the problem of evil vanishes.

III

The reader may want to raise a number of objections. Let me consider two of these.

Admittedly, it is impossible that the Almighty should place everybody, or for that matter anybody, in a state better than which is inconceivable. Yet He could improve the state of everybody and make it better than it is now. The problem of evil may thus be stated not as the problem of why things are not so good that they could not be better, but why things are not better than they actually are.

The answer is that one is justified in complaining about an existing state of affairs only if what one is complaining about is not logically inherent in every state of affairs, that is, if the situation could be changed into another in which the reason for complaint would be removed. If, however, it is clear now that no matter what changes are introduced, in any new situation there is exactly as much reason to complain as before, then there is no right to demand that the old situation be replaced by another. In our case it is clear that, no matter by how much the degree of desirability of the state of an individual be increased, it would still be just as short as it is now of being so large that larger it could not be. Therefore, in any improved situation, there is objectively as much reason for complaint as in the present situation. So while the situation of creatures could be so changed as to make them cease to complain, nothing could be done to mitigate the objective situation and remove the objective grounds on which to complain, namely, that things are less good than they could be. The reason for this complaint remains constant through all changes; there is, therefore, no objective justification for demanding any changes.

Another objection a sceptic might want to raise is that while nobody can reach the logical limit of happiness, there seem to be no conceptual obstacles against at least eliminating all possible misery. He could therefore challenge the theist and say that if God were good, then at least He should not have permitted any creature, however exalted or humble its kind, to be positively distressed at any time.

But once we have agreed on the reasonableness of the value judgment expounded in the previous section, it necessarily follows that it is possible for A to be really much better off than B even though A is dissatisfied and B satisfied. For A, who may be deficient in one of the ingredients that contribute to the desirability of his condition—namely in happiness, may have been more than sufficiently compensated by having been granted the other ingredient in abundance, i.e., by having been allotted a much higher rank in the hierarchy of beings. Thus we can see the absurdity of the sceptic's position. Confronted with B, he sees no grounds to question Divine goodness, since B does not suffer. But should God *improve* B's lot and raise the degree of the desirability of his state to be equal to that of A, this he would regard as evil!

I shall not discuss here any more objections[2] but point out that it is not surprising that upon hearing my solution for the first time the reader should feel a certain amount of uneasiness. This is to a certain degree due to the fact that it seems paradoxical that an omnipotent being is capable of doing less than a human being, that is, that the former cannot, while the latter can, follow the important ethical rule to increase everybody's degree of desirability of state to the utmost of one's ability. In fact, however, this should not look so strange when we remember that it is also true that an omnipotent being, unlike a human being, is incapable of putting together a weight which he cannot lift.

Another source of dissatisfaction may be the fact that my solution offers no solace for another one's grief. Indeed, it would be most callous of me to tell a victim of a series of disasters, "You have no grounds for lamentation. Even if nothing unpleasant had ever happened, in which case you would not be complaining, objectively speaking you would still be as far from having the maximum degree of desirability of state as you are now. So what is the point of your complaints?" It must, however, be realized that the important psychological task of providing comfort for the sufferer and the logical task of demonstrating the failure of the alleged proof of the inconsistency of theism are two different tasks. It may well be that the first task is more urgently needed. Still, defending theism against the attempt to dismiss it as incoherent has value of its own.

Notes

1. Some people fail to realize this simple truth. There are theologians who have claimed that the unprecedented atrocities of Auschwitz have created unsurmountable difficulties for theism, which now needs to be revised radically. Now, admittedly, the horrors of Auschwitz are unprecedented, but this has no effect on the status of the problem of evil. Either we can show that suffering is not incompatible with divine goodness and, therefore, the problem does not arise in any possible situation, or we cannot, in which case the slightest amount of suffering creates a problem.

2. I discuss ten objections in chapter 10 of my *Religion and Scientific Method* (D. Reidel, 1977).

FIVE

WHY DOES GOD HIDE HIS EXISTENCE?

Michael J Murray

> *But if I go to the east, he is not there;*
> *if I go to the west I do not find him.*
> *When he is at work in the north, I do not see him;*
> *when he turns to the south, I catch no glimpse of him.*
> —Job 23:8–9

I

The sentiments expressed by Job in the above epigram are ones that have been expressed by the sophisticated atheist as well as the typical church-goer. Most of us, in fact, have wondered at one time or another why it is that God does not reveal Himself in some dramatic fashion if He actually exists. Yet, while this question is widely entertained, it has received surprisingly little attention in the philosophical literature. In addition to puzzling many theists, the fact of divine hiddenness has prompted some non-theists to challenge the theists to provide some explanation for God's apparent silence. The problem they have raised can be roughly stated as follows: If, as most theists claim, belief in God is essential to ultimate human fulfillment, one would expect that God would provide us with unambiguous evidence for His existence. However, such evidence is not forthcoming. Therefore, it is unlikely that the theist's God exists.

The atheist Norwood Russell Hanson makes this case

against the theist as follows in his essay "What I Do Not Believe":

> . . . 'God exists' *could* in principle be established for all factually—it just happens not to be, certainly not for everyone! Suppose, however, that next Tuesday morning, just after breakfast, all of us in this one world are knocked to our knees by a percussive and ear-shattering thunderclap. Snow swirls; leaves drop from the trees; the earth heaves and buckles; buildings topple and towers tumble; the sky is ablaze with an eerie, silvery light. Just then, as all the people of this world look up, the heavens open—the clouds pull apart—revealing an unbelievably immense and radiant-like Zeus figure, towering above us like a hundred Everests. He frowns darkly as lightning plays across the features of his Michelangeloid face. He then points down—*at* me!—and explains, for every man and child to hear:
>
> 'I have had quite enough of your too-clever logic-chopping and word-watching in matters of theology. Be assured, N. R. Hanson, that I most certainly do exist.'
>
> . . . Please do not dismiss this as a playful, irreverent Disney-oid contrivance. The conceptual point here is that *if* such a remarkable event were to occur, *I* for one should certainly be convinced that God does exist. That matter of fact would have been settled once and for all time. . . That god exists would, through this encounter, have been confirmed for me and for everyone else in a manner every bit as direct as that involved in any non-controversial factual claim.[1]

Hanson's point, of course, is that since God has not produced such a theophany, we not only lack good evidence that such a God exists, but that this heavenly silence actually inveighs against God's existence. The argument is made even more forcefully by Nietzsche in the following section:

A God who is all-knowing and all powerful and who does not even make sure his creatures understand his intention—could that be a god of goodness? Who allows countless doubts and dubieties to persist, for thousands of years, as though the salvation of mankind were unaffected by them, and who on the other hand holds out the prospect of frightful consequences if any mistake is made as to the nature of truth? Would he not be a cruel god if he possessed the truth and could behold mankind miserably tormenting itself over the truth?—But perhaps he is a god of goodness notwithstanding—and merely *could* express himself more clearly! Did he perhaps lack the intelligence to do so? Or the eloquence? So much the worse! For them he was perhaps also in error as to that which he calls his 'truth', and is himself not so very far from being the 'poor deluded devil'! Must he not then endure almost the torments of Hell to have to see his creatures suffer so, and go on suffering even more through all eternity, for the sake of knowledge of him, and *not* be able to help and counsel them, except in the manner of a deaf and dumb man making all kinds of ambiguous signs when the most fearful danger is about to befall on his child or his dog? . . . All religions exhibit traces of the fact that they owe their origin to an early, immature intellectuality in man—they all take astonishingly *lightly* the duty to tell the truth: they as yet know nothing of a *Duty of God* to be truthful towards mankind and clear in the manner of his communications.[2]

The challenge to the theists is to explain this heavenly silence.

II

In order to understand the nature of the problem of divine hiddenness it is important to ask exactly what the objector to theism finds problematic here. The real problem, as I see it, is the fact that the hiddenness of God seems to be closely tied to disbelief. For most Christian theists, disbelief is a form of sin, possibly the most damaging form. As a result, the problem appears to reduce to the fact that God's self-imposed obscurity seems to be indirectly, or possibly directly, responsible for an important form of evil.[3] The atheist's challenge, then, amounts to this: why has God established conditions, or at least allowed conditions to prevail, which seem to lead to the occurrence of a significant amount of evil, especially evil of such a grave sort? Seen in this way, the problem is similar to a number of others which fall under the traditional problem of evil. One might thus be led to consider, first, whether or not the hiddenness of God might simply be treated as a species of the problem of evil and thus be resolved by appealing to certain traditional theodicies regarding this problem. What I intend to show here is that certain traditional theodicies do seem to provide some interesting resolutions to the problem of God's hiddenness. I will begin in this section with a discussion of the traditional free-will defense and show how it can be brought to bear on this vexing problem.

Briefly, a free-will theodicy claims that the existence of free-will causes, allows, or presupposes the possibility of certain evils. However, there are two distinct species of free-will theodicies, both of which I will make use of in the course of this discussion. The first type of free-will theodicy argues that one of the consequences of endowing creatures with free-will is that these beings have the option to choose evil over good. As a result, it is impossible that God actualize a world such that there are both free beings and also no possibility of these beings undertaking evil actions. I call theodicies of this type *consequent free-will theodicies*. They are "consequent" in the sense that evil is to be accounted for in terms of conditions that arise as a consequence of the existence of free-will in our world. It is this sort of theodicy that is most often invoked by theists in order to account for the existence of moral evil in the world.

However, the type of free-will theodicy I am going to be concerned with first is somewhat different. The theodicy that is important here argues that there are certain *antecedent* conditions that must necessarily hold or fail to hold if beings endowed with freedom are to be able to exercise this freedom in a morally significant manner. For example, Swinburne, and others, have argued that any world which is such that free beings can exercise their freedom in a morally significant manner must also be a world in which there are stable natural regularities of some sort. If this were not the case, it is argued, free creatures could never come to understand that there are regular connections between their undertakings and the consequence of their undertakings. So, for example, if there were no stable natural regularities, firing a gun at another person's head at point-blank range may, on one occasion, give them a haircut, whereas on another occasion it may kill them. But it seems clear that one could not be said to be morally responsible for their actions if they had no way of knowing that their undertaking, in this case firing the gun, would have the undesirable consequence of taking another life. As a result, free creatures must be created in a world in which such stable connections between undertakings and the consequences of undertakings obtain. And it seems plausible to suppose that such a world requires a set of stable natural regularities to insure the stability of this very connection. It is only when we can be assured that, for example, gun-firings result in certain predictable consequences, that we can be responsible for the outcomes of such actions.

However, the argument continues, the existence of stable natural laws may also lead to other events which result in natural evil, for example, hurricanes, earthquakes, and so on. Thus, if one can argue that there is some overriding reason why God should create a world with beings that are free and also able to exercise that freedom in a morally significant fashion, then the existence of these laws which give rise to natural evil are justified.

This argument strategy thus contends that certain antecedent conditions must obtain if free creatures are to be able to exercise their freedom in the most robust sense. And since there is good reason for creating creatures who can exercise their freedom in this fashion, there is good reason to create the necessary antecedent conditions which would allow for such exercising of freedom. One can then argue that even though certain evil states of affairs might result from these antecedent conditions obtaining, such is necessary if God is going to be able to bring about the greater good of actualizing a world in which free creatures can exercise their freedom in a thoroughly robust manner.

Clearly, theodicies of this sort differ from theodicies of the consequent type in that they argue that there are certain antecedent conditions which are requisite for free beings to be able to exercise their freedom and that such conditions may incidentally lead to certain other evil states of affairs. However, it is argued, the circumstances for which these antecedent conditions are necessary are sufficiently good to justify the evil which arises as a result of their obtaining. I will refer to this class of theodicies as *antecedent free-will theodicies*.

In addition to arguing that certain conditions must *obtain* for free creatures to be able to exercise their freedom, it can also be shown that certain conditions must *fail to obtain* if free beings are to be able to exercise their freedom in a morally significant manner. Specifically, it appears that one cannot act freely when one is in the condition of *compulsion by another in the context of a threat*. Under conditions that I will specify below, it seems clear that fully robust and morally significant free-will cannot be exercised by someone who is compelled by another in the context of a threat. Further, I will argue that if God does not remain "hidden" to a certain extent, at least some of the free creatures He creates would be in the condition of being compelled in the context of a threat and, as a result, such creatures could not exercise their freedom in this robust, morally significant manner.

It seems at least *prima facie* plausible to claim that morally significant freedom cannot be exercised by an individual who is being told to perform a certain action in the context of a significant threat, say, hand over his money to one holding a gun to his head and threatening to shoot. . . .

III

There is, however, an ambiguity regarding exactly what constitutes a "significant threat." Not just any threat counts as a compelling one since, for example, one would not feel compelled to hand their money over to a robber who simply threatened to call them a dirty word. What would be helpful is a list of necessary and sufficient conditions which would suffice to clarify exactly what constitutes a threat significant enough to eliminate the possibility of morally significant, rational freedom. Unfortunately, the subject matter here does not allow for such precision. However, there are certain factors which jointly determine "threat significance." Below I will discuss these factors in an effort to provide a clearer picture of how threats give rise to compulsion and how this compulsion affects the exercise of morally significant free-will.

The three factors that are important for my analysis are what I will call *threat strength, threat imminence,* and *wantonness of the threatened.* By threat strength I mean the degree to which the threatened person feels the consequences of the threat to be harmful to him. By threat imminence I mean the degree to which the threatened perceives that the threat will inevitably follow given that the conditions for the threatened consequences being enacted are met. The notion of "inevitably follows" is ambiguous here and intentionally so. Below I will explain that this notion must be carefully unpacked since the notion of threat imminence is multi-faceted. Finally, by wantonness of the threatened I have in mind a characteristic of the individual threatened to disregard personal well-being in the fact of threats to his freedom. My claim is that the degree of compulsion is *directly proportional* to threat strength and imminence and *inversely proportional* to wantonness. I will now discuss these conditions in more careful detail.

It should be obvious that the degree of compulsion is directly proportional to the degree of threat strength. The degree to which I feel compelled to do an act that I would not otherwise do (say, to give all my money to a stranger) would be much greater if the threatener held a gun to my back than if he threatened to call me a dirty word if I failed to comply with his wish.

It is more difficult to see exactly how threat imminence relates to compulsion simply because it is less easy to characterize. By examining a few cases I think it will become clear that the notion of the consequences of a threat "inevitably following" when the threatened fails to satisfy the conditions of a threat must be cashed out in more than one way. There are, in fact, at least three distinct senses of threat imminence which must be distinguished for my purposes.

The first type of threat imminence is what I will call *probabilistic* threat imminence. Consider the standard robber case above in which I am threatened with being shot if I fail to hand over my wallet to the thief. In this case I would consider it highly probable that the thief would shoot me if I failed to comply with the conditions of the threat. As a result, the probabilistic threat imminence would be high in this case. However, consider another case in which certain prisoners are allowed to spend recreation time in an enclosed prison yard. Surrounding the yard are high barbed wire fences which are periodically punctuated by guard towers. The prisoners have been told that the guards have orders to shoot if any of the prisoners attempt to escape. As a result we have a case which, in important respects, is similar to the standard robber case. Most importantly, in both cases the threatened individuals are under a threat of the same strength, namely, being shot if the conditions of the threat are not satisfied. However, in the prison-yard case, a prisoner might be more tempted to attempt to escape because he might feel that there is some significant probability that the threat would not be successfully carried out because, for example, the guards might miss him at that distance, or because they may fail to see him since they are so busy watching the other prisoners. Thus, in this case the degree of compulsion is somewhat lower than in the standard robber case because the *probability* that the threat will be carried out is somewhat less even though the threat strength is identical.

The second type of threat imminence is what I call *temporal* threat imminence. With this type of threat imminence, compulsion is greater in those cases in which the threat will be carried out with more temporal immediacy, once the conditions of the threat have not been met. To show this consider the standard robber case once again. In such a case the temporal threat imminence is high since I know that if I fail to comply with the robber's demands I will be shot on the spot. Compare this, however, to a case in which the robber tells me that he has a blow gun with darts which he will shoot at me if I fail to hand over my money. Furthermore, the robber tells me that these darts contain a poison which has no antidote and will lead to my certain death in fifty years. In the former case, compulsion is higher because the *temporal imminence* of the threat is greater.[4] Differing degrees of temporal threat imminence may also explain phenomena such as the fact that some individuals choose to eat high fat foods which they know, in the long run, are very likely to cause, say, fatal arteriosclerosis, while these same individuals would not ingest antifreeze, which although quite sweet tasting, is very likely to be immediately fatal. Ingesting both types of substances makes death likely; but ingesting high fat foods makes death likely sometime in the future, whereas ingesting ethylene glycol makes death immediately likely.

Finally, there is *epistemic* threat imminence. This type of imminence is also quite difficult to characterize but it is one with which I believe that we are all familiar. It is this third type of imminence that explains why we believe that massive advertising campaigns are effective in reducing the incidence of smoking or drinking and driving. In both of these cases it seems that few engaging in the behaviors really believe that it is not bad for them; they are usually quite well aware that they are so. Clearly, then, the purpose of such advertising campaigns is not to *inform* the individuals engaging in these behaviors that they are bad for them. What then is their purpose? It can only be to make the fact that these behaviors are dangerous more *epistemically forceful*. Somehow, by repeating the message over and over we become more powerfully aware of just how harmful such behaviors potentially are. As a result, the more epistemically forceful the danger is, the more likely we are to not act in such a way. Likewise, when we are discussing compulsion, the more epistemically imminent a threat, the more compelled the threatened individual will feel.

However, these two factors of strength and imminence alone are not sufficient to explain compulsion by another in the context of a threat completely. This is evident when we look again at our prison-yard case. Why, one might wonder, do certain prisoners try to escape, while others in similar circumstances do not, even though threat strength and imminence are the same for all prisoners? Assuming that none of them wishes to remain in prison, why do they not all try to escape? This question points to the need for a third factor, and this factor is the wantonness of the threatened. Again, this factor is difficult to define precisely. However, it does seem clear that different individuals under the same threat and with the same degree of threat imminence can feel compelled to different degrees depending on a certain internal character trait which can be described as incorrigibility or threat indifference. This trait can be roughly characterized as a feeling of indifference for one's well-being in cases where that well-being is threatened should there be a refusal to submit to the terms of some restriction on one's freedom.

These, then, are the factors which must be taken into account when we consider the degree to which a threat prevents the exercise of robust morally significant freedom. While it is surely impossible to quantify these characteristics in order to define exactly what constitutes a threat which overwhelms freedom, it can be said that the degree to which freedom is compromised is directly proportional to threat strength and imminence and inversely proportional to wantonness.

IV

One feature of the major Western theistic traditions is that they seem to involve the issuing of both temporal and eternal threats for disobedience to the divine will. Passages from, for example, the Hebrew and Christian scriptures, such as the following, represent both aspects of this threatened punishment: "A man who remains stiff-necked after many rebukes will suddenly be destroyed—without remedy" (Prov. 29:1) and "But because of your stubbornness and your unrepentant heart you are storing up wrath against yourself for the day of God's wrath." (Rom. 2:5) As a result, those who are aware of such threats and are convinced of their veracity are in a state where their freedom is at risk. What this creates, simply, is some degree of compulsion by another in the context of the threat. Specifically, it is compulsion by God in the context of a threat of both temporal and eternal punishment. Consequently, on the picture painted by these traditions, God has issued threats, both temporal and eternal, which will be carried out if one fails to submit to Him, in action or belief, in certain ways.[5] Here I will focus particularly on the Christian tradition and the notion of a threat contained therein.

Since these appear to be quite significant threats, the theist must provide some explanation for how this threat can be mitigated so as to prevent the compromising of human freedom. To do this, one of the three factors of compulsion must be mitigated in some way. I will now look at each one to see where the force of compulsion could be averted.

Certainly, with regard to the factor of threat strength, the threat posed by the prospect of eternal damnation is equal to the strongest imaginable threat. One, of course, might wonder why God does not simply eliminate the threat of hell for disobedience and in doing so eliminate or severely limit the threat strength and thus the compulsion. This is an interesting question but not one I will address here. My goal here is to determine whether the traditional, orthodox Christian position can be reconciled with the fact that God does not reveal himself in the manner Hanson might wish. Since the existence of hell is, I take it, a presumption of the traditional Christian view, I will take it for granted at this point. By doing so, however, we also preclude the possibility of mitigating compulsion by attenuating threat strength.

As a result, unless one of the other two factors can be appropriately controlled, it would seem that morally significant exercise of human free-will would be precluded. What about wantonness? It is unlikely that this factor will provide what is required to avoid the consequence of compulsion which eliminates free-will. The reason for this is that it seems likely that the development and functioning of traits such as wantonness is something which falls within the domain of the freedom of the individual. To attempt to argue for this claim in any complete way would lead into the complex psychological

question of whether such personality traits in general are ac-
quired by heredity, environment or elements of individual free
choice. Another area that would need to be addressed is how
we develop character traits relating to wantonness. Aristotelian
views on the development of virtues by the willful cultivation
of habits of right-acting, for example, would support the view
I hold above in my claim that wantonness is a factor that God
cannot manipulate if He desires to preserve free-will. As a
result, my claim is that if God were to preserve human free-
will, manipulating this element of the picture would not be an
option.

This leaves us with the possibility of controlling the degree
of threat imminence. Let's begin by looking at *probabilistic*
threat imminence. This condition seems to provide little help
since, on the Christian story, it is nothing less than certain that
the threat will be carried out if the conditions of the threat are
not met.

What about *temporal* threat imminence? Clearly this condition has some relevance to our case since carrying out the
threat does not follow immediately upon failure to obey the
conditions of the threat. There is no trap door to hell that
opens upon one's first sin or willful failure to assent to the
Christian plan of redemption. Yet merely reducing the temporal imminence of the threat does not appear to be sufficient
guarantee that the creature's freedom is not compromised by
divine compulsion. Given the strength of the threat involved it
does not seem that merely delaying the carrying out of the
threat temporally is sufficient to mitigate compulsion. If it
were, it appears that we should be content to say that God
could appear in the sky, *a la* Hanson, issuing the relevant temporal and eternal threats, and yet not have the actions of free
creatures be compelled by the issuing of such threats. Yet, it
seems that the actions of such free creatures clearly *would be*
compelled if they were to be confronted by such obvious
threats.

We are left then with *epistemic* threat imminence as the final factor which can be attenuated if God desires to preserve the exercise of morally significant freedom by creatures. My claim is that the hiddenness of God is required in order for free beings to be able to exercise their freedom in a morally significant manner given the strength of the threat implied by knowledge of the threat implicit in the traditional Christian story. If God revealed his existence in a more perspicuous fashion we would be in a situation very much like the one in the standard robbery case, i.e., strong threat strength and strong threat imminence such that the level of wantonness of most, if not all, individuals would not significantly diminish their feeling compelled to act in accordance with the demand of the threatener. However, if God desires that there be individuals with free-will who can use it in morally significant ways, then He must decrease the threat imminence of eternal and temporal punishment and He, in fact, does so by making the existence of the threat epistemically ambiguous. It is this epistemic ambiguity that we call the problem of the hiddenness of God.

This may make it clear why God does not, say, open the sky and give a world-wide unambiguous proclamation of his existence. However, it does not seem to explain why there is *the particular degree* of divine hiddenness that there is. An objector may reply here that God may not be able to "open the sky" without the loss of morally significant freedom on the part of humans; yet, must that also mean that merely one more unit of divine manifestation in the world would cause the fabric of significant moral freedom to collapse? The answer is no. What this argument is intended to provide is a response to the question of why God does not provide a grand, universal display of general revelation.[6] But why then does God provide the fairly low general level of revelation that he does? Since God is concerned with preserving the freedom of each individual, the level of general revelation must be such as not to preclude the possibility of anyone's exercising his or her free-will in a morally significant fashion. Since threat strength is constant, God must tailor the degree of general revelation to the individual most likely to be compelled by a threat, namely, the least wanton individual. If this is correct, the degree of threat imminence, and consequently the degree of divine manifestation in the world, must be appropriately moderated. And, the degree of moderation here is likely to be great, with the result that the amount of unambiguous general revelation that God can provide is likely to be fairly minimal.

Notes

1. Norwood Russell Hanson, *What I Do Not Believe and Other Essays* (New York: Humanities Press, 1971), pp. 313–14.

2. Friedrich Nietzsche, *Daybreak*, trans. R. J. Hollingdale (Cambridge: Cambridge University Press, 1982), pp. 89–90. I thank Leon Galis for this quote.

3. In fact, disbelief may be the worst form of evil since its presence can, according to traditional Christian theism, lead to one's being eternally damned.

4. Some have objected to this illustration of the role of temporal imminence since, they argue, the difference between the standard case and the blowgun case is really a matter of threat strength. In the robber case I stand to lose the remainder of my life if I fail to comply whereas in the blowgun case I will still be able to live most of the rest of my life, missing only a little of it. Thus, what I stand to lose in the robber case is much greater and that is why I feel compelled in that case. This may be so, but I believe that other cases can be constructed which make the temporal imminence feature much more salient. To show this consider the following two cases. In the first case a would-be robber tells me that if I fail to hand over my money he has an extremely powerful cattle-prod which will deliver a shock so severe that, while it will not kill me, will cause me extreme pain as well as a short but painful two-week hospital stay. In this case I suspect that failure to comply with the threat will lead to an immediate shock-experience. Compare this to a case in which the would-be robber tells me that he has a delayed-action cattle prod

which delivers the same shock but the shock that it delivers is such that it will not actually experience the shock sensation and two-week disability for fifty years. It seems to me that the result is the same here, namely, that the degree to which I feel compelled is greater in the case with the higher temporal imminence.

5. I put the matter this way so as not to take a stand on the relation between performing good works, faith, and salvation.

6. By general revelation I have in mind revelation given to all, or a very large number of, individuals.

SIX

IS GOD VAIN?

Charles Taliaferro

An objection to theism which has received scant attention in the literature may be called the problem of divine vanity. It may be argued that Christian theism exults in a view of God as vain, egoistic, pompous. The problems of vanity arises in three general (broad) areas, creation, worship, and redemption. With respect to creation, God's bringing into existence creatures in His likeness is akin to bringing into being self-portraits, which is hardly a humble undertaking. God appears to be a super Narcissus who delights in His own reflection. Worship seems inescapably egoistic. God has not only created images of Himself, but expects these images to worship Him, to recount many of His greatest deeds, to be abased before the Divine glory and adore Him. We are even commanded to worship none other than God. Similarly, in salvation history God insists upon being at the center stage. Creaturely moral failure is offensive to the Creator. But instead of creatures succeeding in effecting reconciliation, God Himself does so. God may have taken on human flesh to bring about redemption, but it is still God *qua* divine and human ego who is the principal saving agent. God wants to be the talk of the town.

The problem of vanity may be considered a part of the

general problem of evil as well as a problem for Christian ethics generally. It is part of the problem of evil in that it appears to attribute to God what Christians take to be a vice. Christians imagine God to be completely good, morally perfect and supreme, whereas the charge of the vanity objection is that He is morally inferior to His saints. This creates a problem for a Christian ethic charging us to be perfect even as our heavenly Father is perfect. If we follow our Maker's example, we find ourselves condemned by the Christian understanding of God's ordinances. God appears to flaunt preeminently the very vice God is said to abhor. I begin with preliminary reflections on the relationship between pride and humility and then address the problem of vanity under the headings creation, worship and redemption.

Pride and Humility

Vanity is a form of pride. Christian ethical tradition is united in its condemnation of vanity, but it has not always condemned pride *qua* self-respect or proportionate self-regard. Common parlance appears to support a distinction between acceptable and unacceptable pride; it even reflects a quite positive approval of natural pride. Thus, in the use of the expression "false pride," there is some suggestion that real, true pride is appropriate. "False pride" is this proportionate pride in appearance only, in the same fashion as "false humility" and "false friends" are humility and friends only in appearance. When someone has false pride they have passed beyond proportionate self-regard or respect and landed themselves in egocentrism, vanity, self-aggrandizement. Even so, ordinary language is ambivalent on the matter and "pride" simpliciter may stand for either proportionate or disproportionate self-regard, a term of approval or condemnation. Ethicists have identified the former as natural or proper pride. . . . [I]t consists in feeling a proportionate amount of pleasure in one's undertakings, character or relationships. Vanity involves excessive, disproportionate delight as when one takes enormous pleasure in one's appearance, a pleasure which eclipses any appreciation of others, and so on. . . .

Vain pride and natural pride may range over many areas. One may take pride in one's scope of power, some characteristic or undergoing or even some relationship which is believed to be positive. Likewise one may have humility with respect to some relationship, characteristic, quality, degree of power or undergoing which is believed to be positive. A marked difference between the prideful and humble is that the humble person is aware of the limited nature of these features. As it happens, two people may have identical features, both having the same degree of intellectual prowess say, and yet one has pride in the degree attained whereas the other is humble in appreciating the modesty of that degree [she recognizes the comparative paltry value of such intellectual achievement over against the witness of saints]. In this example we can see the close proximity of humility and proper pride. It may even be that a steadfast refusal to feel proper pride could stem from a misunderstanding of humility. A humble person may be one who knows (or has justified beliefs) that she has qualities of a certain sort and no better, but she does not thereby deny that she has the limited qualities she enjoys.

Two further aspects of pride and humanity may be noted before treating the objection from vanity. First, while pride seems to be incompatible with feeling sorrow or pain in the feature one is proud about, humility is compatible with feeling such sorrow. If we are proud of getting a grant, it cannot be what we take sorrow or feel unmitigated pain and dismay over the windfall. However, if we feel humility about our moral character, having a vivid sense of past and future failings, it is possible to feel unmitigated pain and dismay over these failings. Humility need not involve pain and sorrow in this sense, but it is compatible with it. Second, pride, whether natural or unnatural, appears to involve some kind of self-regard or self-reflection in an essential way. To be proud that X occurs must involve some belief or attitude relating oneself to X. I cannot be proud of the moon unless I have some belief or attitude tying myself and the moon together, however attenuated the tie.[1] Thus, I may be proud that *my* God made it or that it is part of *my* universe. Humility may involve self-reference, indeed a poignant, sharp self-awareness. But it might also be that the humble person is very unself-conscious. One who is humble may have 'died to self' and have a marked self-disregard or self-forgetfulness of the kind some of us have only rarely as when we 'lose ourselves in a book' and the like.

Initially it is difficult indeed to imagine that the God of Christianity could be humble. God is conceived of as limitless in power and knowledge, the principal Creator of all, morally perfect, and unsurpassable in all perfection. Surely it is hard to be humble if you are God, and still harder to imagine the God of Christendom is humble when one considers the specific teachings examined below of creation, worship and redemption. Recall the refrain of a popular country song: "its hard to be humble, when you're perfect in every way." We reproach each other with the accusation that so-and-so acts with a "holier than thou" attitude or "she thinks she is God." But what of the moral fiber of a being who actually *is* holier than ourselves? . . .

Creation

Creation of Divine image bearers as traditionally conceived may appear to be the height of vanity. God is pictured as creating the cosmos for his own glory and creatures are brought into being who are images or reflections of God. They are even called to so act that they come into an increasing likeness to their Maker. Certainly this suggests an extraordinary delight in self. The iconography of pride identifies the mirror as one of vanity's principal instruments. Isn't the Christian God one who loves His own reflection so much that creation is but His looking glass?

The critic may urge further that an appeal to God as Trinity does not suffice to avoid the objection from vanity. The triune life of God might appear to be a supreme model of other-regarding love and self-donation. The Father, Son and Holy Spirit are continuously united in will, forever expressing loving regard for the other. However this is spelled out, the objection of vanity can be raised in terms of the vanity of the Trinity itself. After all, a club of three members might behave in a chauvinistic, aggressively self-concerned manner even though each member of the club behaves in a perfectly other-regarding fashion to his or her fellow member. Similarly, the objection from vanity is not altered by recent discussion as to whether creation by God is voluntary as a freely chosen act or necessary as an act which was free only in the sense of being not forced by a third party, but otherwise was a necessary manifestation of God's nature as goodness.[2] All such discussion might settle is the quandary whether Divine vanity is a freely elected vice or that God is vain by His very nature.

I think that the objection from vanity is less forceful with respect to creation than with respect to worship and redemption. Briefly, a reply to the critic lies in a fuller appreciation of the nature of creation, the metaphysical distinction between God and creatures, and what is meant by being created in God's image.

If classic Christian metaphysics is correct, then God is the only causal agent who could be responsible for there being a contingent cosmos at all. It is a necessary condition of the existence of any contingent object that God exercises his creative conserving power sustaining it in existence. For God to lovingly interact with another, He must create it. Presumably

both loving another and acting haughtily before another requires that the other be created and conserved by God. Bare
creation and conservation of a being does not entail God is
vain. God was not in the position of excluding lots of other
gods from creating, failing to wait His turn in line. . . . Likewise it appears that neither God's failing to create nor creating
entail God is vain. Just as creating may well be a necessary
condition to loving, other-regarding encounter, so failing to
create need not entail God is vain, for while God as trinity
may (as the critic charges) image some ghastly mutual self-
congratulatory club, it certainly need not do so. We can imagine treating the triune Godhead as a society of love in which
other-regardingness reigns and, while accompanied by proper
pride insofar as there is genuine delight in the relations and
features of Godhood, it is not in excess (one is hard pressed to
imagine excess here) and such self-delight is hardly a matter of
harming possible creatures. Failing to create does not entail
God is vain. Nor is it the case that God is vain because He
creates.

But why create in one's own image? Not everything in the
created order is characterized as a divine image; there are rivers,
mountains, volcanoes, and rocks. Only in the biological world,
and specifically among sentient, thinking, active beings do we
find any singling out of creatures who are Divine image bearers.
And it is here that we may note the marked difference between
a creature painting endless self-portraits and the Divine creating
in His image. In the latter case, God brings into existence
agents, creative beings distinct from Himself. Self-portraits do
not love or hate their Maker and their fellow God-portraits.
Our self-portraits do not hate and love, nor possess emotions in
any literal sense. Creatures who are thinking, feeling agents bear
a marked similarity to their creator, but it is in precisely the
ways that allow them to have a life in some way independent of
their maker. We, as image bearers, are not unlike Goethe's description in *Faust*, "little gods in the world."

But consider the following objection. Imagine a mad scientist, Arthur, who populates the world with thousands of clones. Despite the fact these clones are able to live in measured independence of Arthur their creator (Arthur the 500th can insult the original Arthur), isn't there something unseemly egoistic about our mad scientist's creation? Is God's creating us in His likeness analogous to Arthur's cloning creatures that resemble himself?

Yes and no. What appears to be unseemly in the thought experiment is that the mad scientist's cloning amounts to his producing creatures who narrowly resemble himself, in gender, size, race, weight and personality features. Whatever their subsequent exercise of free will, the Arthurs are homogeneous; they are modeled after a limited, perhaps flawed, original. If we alter the thought experiment and suppose that Arthur produces a rich variety of creatures, the ego resemblance is lessened and there is less suggestion of egoism in his creative work. God does not have a specific race, gender, size or weight to copy. Divine image bearers are persons, whatever their dimensions. Moreover, it is good for there to be persons, beings that enjoy sensation and desires and who can exercise reason, memory, imagination, and agency. Thus, it is plausible to regard the creation of such beings as good whether it be by Arthur or God. Our resemblance to God consists in our enjoyment of good making powers like agency, the capacity to love and the like; powers enabling us to be co-creators with God. . . .

I conclude that creating other agents is not by itself vain, though it may appear vain if we imagine the Creator has brought them into existence solely to complement and praise Himself. Earlier I noted that one rationale for creation is to glorify God. Insofar as God is glorified simply by there being good, created states of affairs, the problem of vanity does not arise. But what if part of what it means to glorify God is to praise and worship Him? . . .

Worship

If creation alone does not clinch the critic's case, Christian teaching of worship seems to do so. Isn't it the height of Divine egoism to insist creatures worship and praise God?

I place to the side one solution to this charge, namely the view that worship of God is to be understood solely in terms of creaturely regarding behavior. That is, to worship God is simply to behave as good Samaritans or in a Christ-like fashion to others. Surely any full account of Christian worship must take this into account, but I believe that there remains a distinct Christian teaching that God is to be praised and adored, which is not fully reducible to good creature-to-creature ethics

A reply to the objection of vanity may be seen by a fuller appreciation of the nature of God's attributes and the character of worship.

There is an interesting dispute going back to Plato over whether when one loves another, Miriam loving Eric say, Miriam is loving Eric's properties or Eric himself. Eric may well ask Miriam whether she loves him for his wealth or his body or his wit. Would she love him if he lost these? I will not tease out the subtleties of this debate, the puzzles that arise if Miriam were to claim to love Eric independent of any such properties ("Eric, I just love bare particulars," she might say). There are indeed serious problems with delimiting admirable from undesirable forms of conditional and unconditional love. What I wish to note here is that for an Anselmian theist the problem does not arise about whether one would love God if God were to lose one of his perfections. Perhaps it would be a defective form of fickle human love if Miriam ceased loving Eric when he lost his money. The case of God is different, however, for His metaphysical funds cannot be lost. Traditional Anselmian theism holds that God possesses His properties essentially. Thus, God could not but be limitless in power, knowledge and goodness. In fact, the subtle doctrine of Divine simplicity holds that the relationship of divine attributes is so close that a perspicuous theistic metaphysics treats these attributes as distinct only from a creaturely standpoint. Really, the Divine nature is simple, without any parts, and these different Divine features are different only in the sense that the Divine manifests itself differently to the world, in some respects as omniscient knowledge (God's foreknowledge) and omnipotent power (God's providence) and so on. While Eric and Miriam may debate about whether each would love the other if there was a loss of money and health, the Divine object of love cannot (of metaphysical necessity) lose His richness and life.

To worship and adore God involves, in part, delighting in what we take to be the Divine properties. To love God is not to love some guy who happens to be very wise, but it is to love, adore and delight in supreme Wisdom, Goodness, Knowledge and Power. The question does not arise whether we would still worship God if God were to lose Goodness, Wisdom, Knowledge and Power. A being that could lose these in *toto* would simply not be God. Thus, one important point here is that worship is not directed primarily at an ego (or three egos) but at the instantiation to a supreme degree of various perfections. We do not love a Divine bare particular. Compare the dictum about creatures: we should love the sinner and hate the sin. Whatever may be thought about loving sinners, I do not think we can love God without loving the Divine properties. To love and delight in the Divine properties is to love God.

The value of worship may now be better appreciated. Worship of God does not check creaturely narcissism because of fear that a bigger narcissist will be jealous. Rather, in worship one's attention is drawn to the features which make up the Divine Nature and constitute its excellence. It is a good thing for humans to contemplate things of high, even supreme worth. The Divine perfections are limitless and worthy of unending delight and pleasure. There is a beauty to the holiness of God. Conceivably, the prevention of creatures [from] contemplating and adoring the divine properties may even harm them. God's self-love and our worship is not so much a matter of some fellow being lucky enough to get the Divine features while others did not—and we are stuck with delighting in *his* features. Our devotion is to the Divine perfections themselves, coinstantiated supremely in a person and so coinstantiated (or constituted) that no other being could have them. Much Christian spiritual literature draws attention to a kind of disinterested or self-forgetful character in the high adoration of God. W. H. Auden once commented on the Narcissus myth that its lesson lies in Narcissus delighting in the reflection being *his*, and not simply in the features themselves.[3] This may be further illustrated by a complementary case described by Thomas Nagel. Nagel contends that his apprehension of the badness of pain, indeed a pain *he* is feeling, does not rest essentially upon his apprehension that the pain is his own.

> Of course he (a sufferer) wants to be rid of this pain reflectively—not because he thinks it would be good to reduce the amount of pain in the world. But at the same time his awareness of how bad it is doesn't essentially involve the thought that it is his. The desire to be rid of pain has only the pain as its object. This is shown by the fact that it doesn't even require the idea of oneself in order to make sense: if I lacked or lost the conception of myself as distinct from other possible or actual persons, I could still apprehend the badness of pain, immediately.[4]

In a similar vein we may imagine delighting in certain excellences without smug self-reference.

Can God be humble in His self-delight and summoning creatures to enjoy Himself? God knows his great making features with clarity and precision; He could not think of Himself as being just one of the gods, no better than the next god. Return to a point made above about humility. Humility does not seem to be characterized solely or even essentially by having self-degrading views of the self. On the contrary, the entertainment of false beliefs about oneself is typically associated with arrogance (see, for example, "The Parson's Talk," *Canterbury Tales*). It would appear to be an instance of false humility for one to believe worse of oneself in the face of evidence one has positive features. . . . God's self-love may be understood to express proper pride, not vanity.

There is a dictum common to authorities in the Christian spiritual tradition that we are to love God not for what He does for us, the rewards we might gain from it, but to love God for His own sake. Indeed this is true, but as they also note, the reward and fulfillment to be found from a non-reward conscious religious life is great. There is a sense in which such God-love is akin to God's love of Himself as traditionally conceived, for He does not love Himself for rewards like money or enslaving servile creatures. We may not conclude from our discussion of worship that God is vain, for Divine self-love and creaturely love is directed upon the divine excellences and perfection. Such may be in the domain of proper pride, but not egotism and false pride.[5] Insofar as knowledge, power and goodness are real goods and worthy objects of enjoyment, God's love of these features is itself a good. We may understand Divine self-love in a fanciful way as goodness loving itself.

Consider a final objection. When I love God I am loving a person (or three persons), not their properties of goodness *per se* and so on. I love and reverence a person who discloses Himself to me in religious experience. Theistic essentialism is by no means universally accepted. Some hold that God can lose His omnipotence and omniscience, albeit by His own choice. I can still love God even if He should lose these supreme features. Therefore my love of God cannot be accounted for as an intentional attitude directed upon divine properties *per se*.

Reply: Even if we reject the thesis of Divine simplicity and theistic essentialism, it does not follow that worship is not best construed as a delight in the excellences (properties) which do constitute God. One cannot love a bare particular, a thing which has no properties whatever (one reason, I think, is that of metaphysical necessity there cannot be such ontological items). The above critic is correct that worship does not involve sheer disinterested delight in properties *per se*. First, I believe worship of God involves reverencing the *instantiation* of these properties in a person or person-like Being. We delight in there being a supremely wise, good Creator and not simply in there being a Platonic property of Good, Wise Creatorhood. Second, we also adore the Divine lover revealed in our experience, the One who lovingly interacts with us in specific ways. This still does not circumvent the thesis that worship consists in reverent delight in supremely good or great making properties. The Hound of Heaven we may encounter in religious experience comes to us brimming over with delightful properties. . . .[6]

Redemption

The last charge of the objection from vanity I discuss concerns the Christian account of salvation or redemption. The centrality of Christ may suggest to the critic a prima donna god who cannot bear to allow creatures to effect their own salvation. There is a peculiarity in the Gospel accounts of Jesus' sayings. On the one hand He is humble of heart and on the other He attributes to Himself a title and centrality unequalled in human literature. Who has insisted with such emphasis and force upon His centrality to the cosmos as the Christ of

St. John's gospel? Christian claims about Jesus range from cosmology to the deepest recesses of our personality. In all such matters, Christ is to be in the limelight.

I believe the answer to this charge rests, in part, upon what I noted above about creation and worship. If the motivation for creation need not involve narcissistic vanity, neither need the motivation for the re-creation of life in redemption. . . .

As with creation, God alone is in a position to effect the re-creation of life, a restoration, or bringing about for the first time, a life of moral and spiritual health. There is some debate in the Christian tradition as to what means God was able to use in effecting redemption. Some means would seem to be unavailable (e.g., means which involve God's doing violence to innocent creatures, and so on), but, on all the competing theories, there was a fittingness to God's effecting it through incarnation. Does the atonement via incarnation itself suggest vanity? The critic may charge that God cannot leave humanity alone, but egoism prompts Him to take on human flesh as well.

The incarnation or enfleshment of God need not suggest egoism. There is as little suggestion of vanity here as there is in cases of a human lover who longs for and achieves unity with her beloved. But two Christian tenets make it harder to make a case for improper Divine egoism: the teaching of human divinization, and understanding the incarnation as a kind of Divine limiting. . . .

God does not seek to *absorb* other creatures, but to have them be so linked with Him and He with them, that their action is harmonious and inextricably bound together. Recall Jesus' dictum that whoever harms or benefits the most vulnerable, harms or benefits Himself (Matthew 25:40,41). The conjoinment of wills and intent in a divine-human united life is to be one of creativity and rich in value. The divine human identification is to be so tight as to rule out any narrow self-interest or egoism. God's will is for the flourishing of all, in great, ever increasing plenitude. If we are to imagine taking pleasure in oneself in such a relationship it would be to take pleasure in God, and to take pleasure in God would be to take pleasure in God's whole creation. As we are said to dwell in God, God is said to dwell in us and share joy and sorrow. At the heart of most plausible accounts of altruism and compassion there is emphasis upon one person being affected and shaped by the well-being of another. Your plight is of distress to me; you delight in some of my joys. Such sharing and extension of personal concern suggests a richly generous life.[7] Presumably the mutual regard in Divine human life would be heightened considerably beyond the intimacy of any solely human relationships. The psychology of egoism is not in evidence.

While the Christian understanding of the incarnation suggests to the critic a vain God who cannot leave anyone alone, it can also suggest a startling image of self-limiting love. In sin creatures are bereft of God and one another and, *ex hypothesi* (given any of the plausible theories of the atonement), in need of Divine action to effect a healing. The Divine enfleshment may be understood as a way to enhance the scope of human freedom and rich interplay with the supernatural. This means of grace can be thought of as a marked self-limiting of God. . . .

In *Goods and Virtues* Michael Slote comments that humility seems to be of greater value, or to be more wonderful, the more that it is embraced by persons of greater traits and character. Thus:

> But however we are ultimately to analyze humility, it follows from the little we have already said that humility is (in the sense intended) a dependent virtue. For intuitively it seems to attain its full status as a virtue or desirable trait of character only when accompanied by other desirable traits. It is a positive virtue only in someone we have other reasons to think well of. In addition, humility can

seem more wonderful, more admirable, the more highly we regard someone's other traits; . . .[8]

Surely the Divine limiting and the supremely redemptive willingness to be subject to betrayal, hatred and physical suffering may be understood as God embracing a humbled role. The God who comes to us as a servant does not strike one naturally as the god of Narcissus.

In concluding, I concede that for all I have suggested in reply to my imagined critic, at best I have shown that the vanity objection lacks clear force. There are ways to meet the objection. We may succeed in reading the notions of incarnation and divinization in salvation history as involving a real humbling of Godhead. Divine creation and worship are instances of proper pride, not vanity. Moreover, we may appeal to tenets in Christianity which appear to portray God as not in any way having defects which prompt you and me to vain pride, *viz.* low self-image, a need to show off and so on. The critic may still persist, and her persistence may stem from a sound, penetrating psychoanalysis of evil. Evil has many faces. But the critic's persistence may also stem from lack of appreciating the subtleties of the good.[9]

Notes

1. See David Hume, *A Treatise of Human Nature,* Book 2, part 1. For a recent illuminating discussion of this relation see *Pride, Shame and Guilt* by Gabriele Taylor (Oxford: Clarendon, 1985).

2. Cf. Norman Kretzmann, "Goodness, Knowledge, and Indeterminacy in the Philosophy of Thomas Aquinas," *Journal of Philosophy,* October 1983.

3. W. H. Auden cited by Henry Fairlie, *The Seven Deadly Sins Today* (Notre Dame, Ind.: University of Notre Dame, 1979), p. 53.

4. Thomas Nagel, *The View from Nowhere* (New York: Oxford University Press, 1986). p. 161. To use Nagel's terminology, I believe there are agent-relative as well as agent-neutral reasons for Divine

worship. The worth of such worship is appreciable from an impersonal standpoint or the view from nowhere in particular.

5. Immanuel Kant claimed that humility and true, noble pride are two features of proper self-respect. See his *Lectures on Ethics*, "Proper Self-Respect" and "Duties to Oneself," translated by Louis Enfield (New York: Harper and Row, 1963).

6. Of course there are many metaphysical theories about the relationship of properties and things, the qualified particular theory of Douglas Long, the bundled property theory of Bertrand Russell, and the property and bare particular theory of Edwin Allaire. For present purposes I am assuming that whichever metaphysics is adopted, worship is oriented towards certain excellent properties.

7. I seek to develop a religious understanding of this sharing in "The Co-inherence," *Christian Scholar's Review* 18(1989): 333–45. For a recent elucidation of unselfish concern for others, see *Unselfishness* by Nicholas Rescher (Pittsburgh: University of Pittsburgh Press, 1975), especially "The Vicarious Affects and the Modalities of Unselfishness." Current work on altruistic compassion can also illumine the Christian understanding of the spiritual life. See Thomas Nagel's *The Possibility of Altruism* (Princeton: Princeton University Press, 1978) and Lawrence Blum's *Friendship, Altruism and Morality* (Boston: Routledge and K. Paul, 1980). *Egoism and Altruism,* edited by R. D. Milo (Belmont, Calif.: Wadsworth, 1973) is a helpful anthology drawing together important classic work on the topic.

8. Michael Slote, *Goods and Virtues* (Oxford: Clarendon Press, 1983). p. 62.

9. This paper is dedicated to my brother, Robin Taliaferro, who first pressed home to me the force of the objection from vanity.

SEVEN

WHY DOES GOD REQUIRE PRAYER?

Eleonore Stump

Ordinary Christian believers of every period have in general taken prayer to be fundamentally a request made of God for something specific believed to be good by the one praying. The technical name for such prayer is "impetration"; I am going to refer to it by the more familiar designation "petitionary prayer." There are, of course, many important kinds of prayer which are not requests; for example, most of what is sometimes called "the higher sort of prayer"—praise, adoration, thanksgiving—does not consist in requests and is not included under petitionary prayer. But basic, common petitionary prayer poses problems that do not arise in connection with the more comtemplative varieties of prayer, and it is petitionary prayer with its special problems that I want to examine. . . . The cases which concern me in this paper are those in which someone praying a petitionary prayer makes a specific request freely (at least in his own view) of an omniscient, omnipotent, perfectly good God, conceived of in the traditional orthodox way. I am specifying that the prayers are made freely because I want to discuss this problem on the assumption that man has free will and that not everything is predetermined. I am making this assumption, first because I want to examine the problem of petitionary prayer as it arises for ordinary Christian believers, and I think their understanding of the problem typically includes the assumption that man has free will, and secondly because adopting the opposite view enormously complicates the attempt to understand and justify petitionary prayer. If all things are predetermined—and worse, if they are all predetermined by the omnipotent and omniscient God to whom one is praying—it is much harder to conceive of a satisfactory justification for petitionary prayer. One consequence of my making this assumption is that I will not be drawing on important traditional Protestant accounts of prayer such as those given by Calvin and Luther, for instance, since while they may be thoughtful, interesting accounts, they assume God's complete determination of everything.

I think that I can most effectively and plausibly show the problem which interests me by presenting a sketchy analysis of the Lord's Prayer. It is a prayer attributed to Christ himself, who is supposed to have produced it just for the purpose of teaching his disciples how they ought to pray. So it is an example of prayer which orthodox Christians accept as a paradigm, and it is furthermore, a clear instance of petitionary prayer. Consequently, it is a particularly good example for my purposes. In what follows, I want to make clear, I am not concerned either to take account of contemporary Biblical exegesis or to contribute to it. I want simply to have a look at the prayer—in fact, at only half the prayer—as it is heard and prayed by ordinary twentieth-century Christians.

As the prayer is given in Luke 11, it contains seven requests. The last four have to do with the personal needs of those praying, but the first three are requests of a broader sort.

The first, "Hallowed be thy name," is commonly taken as a request that God's name be regarded as holy.[1] I am not sure what it means to regard God's name as holy, and I want to avoid worries about the notion of having attitudes towards God's *name*. All the same, I think something of the following sort is a sensible interpretation of the request. The common

Biblical notion of holiness has at its root a sense of strong separateness.[2] And it may be that to regard God's name as holy is only to react to it very differently from the way in which one reacts to any other name—and that could happen because it seems specially precious or also (for example) because it seems specially feared. On this understanding of the request, it would be fulfilled if everyone (or almost everyone) took a strongly emotional and respectful attitude towards God's name. But it may be that this is too complicated as an interpretation of the request, and that to regard God's name as holy is simply to love and revere it. In that case, the request is fulfilled if everyone or almost everyone regards God's name very reverentially. And there are New Testament passages which foretell states of affairs fulfilling both these interpretations of the request—prophesying a time at or near the end of the world when all men fear or love God's name, and a time when the inhabitants of earth are all dedicated followers of God.[3]

The second request in the Lord's Prayer is that God's kingdom come. Now according to orthodox Judaeo-Christian beliefs, God is and always has been ruler of the world. What then does it mean to ask for the advent of his kingdom? Plainly, there is at least some sense in which the kingdom of heaven has not yet been established on earth and can be waited and hoped for. And this request seems to be for those millennial times when everything on earth goes as it ought to go, when men beat their swords into plowshares (Is. 2:4) and the wolf dwells at peace with the lamb (Is. 11:6, 65:25). This too, then, is a request for a certain state of affairs involving all or most men, the state of affairs at the end of the world prophesied under one or another description in Old and New Testament passages (cf., e.g., Rev. 21:1–4).

And it seems closely related to the object of the third request, "Thy will be done on earth as it is in heaven." There is, of course, a sense in which, according to Christian doctrine, God's will is always done on earth. But that is the sense in which God allows things to happen as they do (God's so-called "permissive will"). God permits certain people to have evil intentions, he permits certain people to commit crimes, and so on, so that he wills to let happen what does happen; and in this sense his will is always done. But in heaven, according to Christian doctrine, it is not that God permits what occurs to occur, and so wills in accordance with what happens, but rather that what happens happens in accordance with his will. So only the perfect good willed unconditionally by God is ever done in heaven. For God's will to be done on earth in such a way, everyone on earth would always have to do only good. This request, then, seems to be another way of asking for the establishment of God's kingdom on earth; and it also seems linked with certain New Testament prophecies—there will be a "new earth," and the righteous meek with inherit it (cf., e.g., Mt. 5:5 and Rev. 5:10 and 21:1–4).

What I think is most worth noticing in this context about all three of these first requests of the Lord's Prayer is that it seems absolutely pointless, futile, and absurd to make them. All three seem to be requests for the millennium or for God's full reign on earth. But it appears from New Testament prophecies that God has already determined to bring about such a state of affairs in the future. And if God has predetermined that there will be such a time, then what is asked for in those three requests is already sure to come. But, then, what is the point of making the prayer? Why ask for something that is certain to come whether you beg for it or flee from it? It is no answer to these questions to say, as some theologians have done,[4] that one prays in this way just because Jesus prescribed such a prayer. That attempt at an answer simply transfers responsibility for the futile action from the one praying to the one being prayed to; it says nothing about what sense there is in the prayer itself. On the other hand, if, contrary to theological appearances, the things prayed for are not predetermined and their occurrence or nonoccurrence is still in doubt, *could* the issue possibly be resolved by someone's asking for one or another outcome? If Jimmy Carter, say (or some other Christian), does not ask for God's kingdom to come, will God therefore fail to establish it? Or will he establish it *just because* Jimmy Carter asked for it, though he would not have done so otherwise? Even Carter's staunchest supporters might well find it frightening to think so; and yet if we do not answer these questions in the affirmative, the prayer seems futile and pointless. So either an omniscient, omnipotent, perfectly good God has predetermined this state of affairs or he hasn't; and either way, asking for it seems to make no sense. This conclusion is applicable to other cases of petitionary prayer as well. To take just one example, suppose that Jimmy Carter prays the altruistic and Christian prayer that a particular atheistic friend of his be converted and so saved from everlasting damnation. If it is in God's power to save that man, won't he do so without Jimmy Carter's prayers? Won't a perfectly good God do all the good he can no matter what anyone prays for or does not pray for? Consequently, either God or his goodness will save the man in any case, so that the prayer is pointless, or there is some point in the prayer but God's goodness appears impugned. . . .

Christian literature contains a number of discussions of the problem with petitionary prayer and various attempts to solve it. For the sake of brevity, I want to look just at the proposed solution Aquinas gives. It is the most philosophically sophisticated of the solutions I know. . . . The basic argument he relies on to rebut various objections against the usefulness of prayer is this. Divine Providence determines not only what effects there will be in the world, but also what causes will give rise to those effects and in what order they will do so. Now human action, too, are causes. "For," Thomas says, "we pray not in order to change the divine disposition but for the sake of acquiring by petitionary prayer what God has disposed to be achieved by prayer."[5]

Perhaps the first worry which this argument occasions stems from the appearance of theological determinism in it: God determines not only what effects there will be but also what the causes of those effects will be and in what order the effects will be produced. It is hard to see how such a belief is compatible with freedom of the will. In the preamble to this argument, however, Thomas says he is concerned *not* to deny free will but, on the contrary, to give an account of prayer which preserves free will. So I want simply to assume that he has in mind some distinction or some theory which shows that, despite appearances, his argument is not committed to a thorough-going determinism, and I am going to ignore any troubles in the argument having to do with the compatibility of predestination or foreknowledge and free will.

For present purposes, what is more troublesome about this argument is that it does not provide any real help with the problem it means to solve. According to Thomas, there is nothing absurd of futile about praying to God, given God's nature, because God has by his providence arranged things so that free human actions and human prayers will form part of the chain of cause and effect leading to the state of the world ordained in God's plan. And so, on Thomas's view, prayer should not be thought of as an attempt to get God to do something which he would not otherwise do but rather as an effort to produce an appropriate and preordained cause which will result in certain effects since God in his providence has determined things to be so. Now surely there can be no doubt that, according to Christian doctrine, God wants men to pray and answers prayers; and consequently it is plain that God's plan for the world includes human prayers as causes of certain effects. The difficulty lies in explaining how such a doctrine makes sense. Why should prayers be included in God's plan as causes of certain effects? And what sense is there in the notion that a perfect and unchangeable God, who disposes and plans everything, fulfills men's prayers asking him to do one thing or another? Thomas's argument, I think, gives no help with these questions and so gives no help with this problem of petitionary prayer.

This argument of Thomas's is roughly similar in basic strategy to other traditional arguments for prayer[6] and is furthermore among the most fully developed and sophisticated arguments for prayer, but it seems to me inadequate to make sense of petitionary prayer. I think, then, that it is worthwhile exploring a sort of argument different from those that stress the connection between God's omniscience or providence and men's prayers. In what follows I want to offer a tentative and preliminary sketch of the way in which such an argument might go.

Judaeo-Christian concepts of God commonly represent God as loving mankind and wanting to be loved by men in return. . . . [T]o say that God loves men and wants to be loved in return is to say something that has a place in philosophical theology and is indispensable to Christian doctrine. Throughout the Old and New Testaments, the type of loving relationship wanted between man and God is represented by various images, for example, sometimes as the relationship between husband and wife, sometimes as that between father and child. And sometimes (in the Gospel of John, for instance) it is also represented as the relationship between true friends.[7] But if the relationship between God and human beings is to be one which at least sometimes can be accurately represented as the love of true friendship, then there is a problem for both parties to the relationship, because plainly it will not be easy for there to be friendship between an omniscient, omnipotent, perfectly good person and a fallible, finite, imperfect person. The troubles of generating and maintaining friendship in such a case are surely the perfect paradigms of which the troubles of friendship between a Rockefeller child and a slum child are just pale copies. Whatever other troubles there are for friendship in these cases, there are at least two dangers for the disadvantaged or inferior member of the pair. First, he can be so overcome by the advantages or superiority of his "friend" that he becomes simply a shadowy reflection of the other's personality, a slavish follower who slowly loses all sense of his own tastes and desires and will. Some people, of course, believe that just this sort of attitude towards God is what Christianity wants and gets from the best of its adherents; but I think that such a belief goes counter to the spirit of the Gospels, for example, and I don't think that it can be found even in such intense mystics as St. Teresa and St. John of the Cross. Secondly, in addition to the danger of becoming completely dominated, there is the danger of becoming spoiled in the way that members of a royal family in a ruling house are subject to. Because of the power at their disposal in virtue of their connections, they often become tyrannical, willful, indolent, self-indulgent, and the like. The greater the discrepancy in status and condition between the two friends, the greater the danger of even inadvertently overwhelming and oppressing or overwhelming and spoiling the lesser member of the pair; and if he is overwhelmed in either of these ways, the result will be replacement of whatever kind of friendship there might have been with one or another sort of using. Either the superior member of the pair will use the lesser as his lackey, or the lesser will use the superior as his personal power source. To put it succinctly, then, if God wants some kind of true friendship with men, he will have to find a way of guarding against both kinds of overwhelming.

It might occur to someone to think that even if we assume the view that God wants friendship between himself and human beings, it does not follow that he will have any of the problems just sketched, because he is omnipotent.[8] If he wants friendship of this sort with men, one might suppose, let him just will it and it will be his. I do not want to stop here to argue against this view in detail, but I do want just to suggest that there is reason for thinking it to be incoherent, at least on the assumption of free will adopted at the beginning of this paper, because it is hard to see how God could bring about such a friendship magically, by means of his omnipotence, and yet permit the people involved to have free will. If he could do so, he could make a person freely love him in the right sort of way, and it does not seem reasonable to think he could do so.[9] On the face of it, then, omnipotence alone does not do away with the two dangers for friendship that I sketched above. But the institution of petitionary prayer, I think, can be understood as a safeguard against these dangers.

It is easiest to argue that petitionary prayer serves such a function in the case of a man who prays for himself. In praying for himself, he makes an explicit request for help, and he thereby acknowledges a need or a desire and his dependence on God for satisfying that need or desire. If he gets what he prayed for, he will be in a position to attribute his good fortune to God's doing and to be grateful to God for what God has given him. If we add the undeniable uncertainty of his getting what he prays for, then we will have safeguards against what I will call (for lack of a better phrase) overwhelming spoiling. These conditions make the act of asking a safeguard against tyrannical and self-indulgent pride, even if the one praying thinks of himself grandly as having God on his side.

We can see how the asking guards against the second danger, of oppressive overwhelming, if we look for a moment at the function of roughly similar asking for help when both the one asking and the one asked are human beings. Suppose a teacher sees that one of his students is avoiding writing a paper and is thereby storing up trouble for himself at the end of the term. And suppose that the student *asks* the teacher for extra help in organizing working time and scheduling the various parts of the work. In that case I think the teacher can without any problem give the student what he needs, provided, of course, that the teacher is willing to do as much for any other student, and so on. But suppose, on the other hand, that the student does not ask the teacher for help and that the teacher instead calls the student at home and simply presents him with the help he needs in scheduling and discipline. The teacher's proposals in that case are more than likely to strike the student as meddling interference, and he is likely to respond with more or less polite variations on "Who asked you?" and "Mind your own business." Those responses, I think, are healthy and just. If the student were having ordinary difficulties getting his work done and yet docilely and submissively accepted the teacher's unrequested scheduling of his time, he would have taken the first step in the direction of unhealthy passivity towards his teacher. And if he and his teacher developed that sort of relationship, he could end by becoming a lackey-like reflection of his teacher. Bestowing at least some benefits only in response to requests for them is a safeguard against such an outcome when the members of the relationship are not equally balanced.

It becomes much harder to argue for this defense of prayer as soon as the complexity of the case is increased even just a little. Take, for example, Monica's praying for her son Augustine. There is nothing in Monica's praying for Augustine which shows that *Augustine* recognizes that he has a need for God's help or that *he* will be grateful if God gives him what *Monica* prays for. Nor is it plain that *Monica's* asking shields Augustine from oppressive overwhelming by God. So it seems as if the previous arguments fail in this case. But consider again the case in which a teacher sees that a student of his could use help but does not feel that he can legitimately volunteer his help unasked. Suppose that John, a friend of that student, comes to see the teacher and says, "I don't know if you've noticed, but Jim is having trouble getting to his term paper. And unless he gets help, I think he won't do it at all and will be in danger of flunking the course." If the teacher now goes to help Jim and is rudely or politely asked "What right have you got to interfere?" he'll say, "Well, in fact, your friend came to me and *asked* me to help." And if John is asked the same question, he will probably reply, "But I'm your friend; I had to do *something.*" I think, then, that because John asks the teacher, the teacher is in a position to help with less risk of oppressive meddling than before. Obviously, he cannot go very far without incurring that risk as fully as before; and perhaps the most he can do if he wants to avoid oppressive meddling is to try to elicit from *Jim* in genuinely uncoercive ways a request for help. And, of course, I chose Monica and Augustine to introduce this case because, as Augustine tells it in the *Confessions*, God responded to Monica's fervent and continued prayers for Augustine's salvation by arranging the circumstances of Augustine's life in such a way that finally Augustine himself freely asked God for salvation.

One might perhaps think that there is something superfluous and absurd in God's working through the intermediary of prayer in this way. If Jim's friend can justify his interference on the grounds that he is Jim's friend and has to do *something*, God can dispense with this sort of petitionary prayer, too. He can give aid unasked on the grounds that he is the *creator* and has to do something. But suppose that Jim and John are only acquaintances who have discussed nothing more than their schoolwork; and suppose that John, by overhearing Jim's phone conversations, has come to believe that all Jim's academic troubles are just symptoms of problems he is having with his parents. If John asks the teacher to help Jim with his personal problems, and if the teacher begins even a delicate attempt to do so by saying that John asked him to do so, he and John could both properly be told to mind their own business. It is not the *status* of his relationship or even the depth of his care and compassion for Jim which puts John in a position to defend himself by saying "But I'm your friend." What protects John against the charge of oppressive meddling is rather the degree to which Jim has freely, willingly, shared his life and thoughts and feelings with John. So John's line of defense against the charge of oppressive meddling can be attributed to God only if the person God is to aid has willingly shared his thoughts and feelings and the like with God. But it is hard to imagine anyone putting himself in such a relation to a person he believes to be omnipotent and good without his also *asking* for whatever help he needs.

Even if the argument can be made out so far, one might be inclined to think that it will not be sufficient to show the compatibility of God's goodness with the practice of petitionary prayer. If one supposes that God brought Augustine to Christianity in response to Monica's prayers, what is one to say about Augustine's fate if Monica had not prayed for him? And what does this view commit one to maintain about people who neither pray for themselves nor are prayed for? It looks as if an orthodox Christian who accepts the argument about petitionary prayer so far will be committed to a picture of this sort. God is analogous to a human father with two very different children. Both Old and New Testaments depict God as doing many good things for men without being asked to do so, and this human father, too, does unrequested good things for both his children. But one child, who is healthy and normal, with healthy, normal relations to his father, makes frequent requests of the father which the father responds to and in virtue of which he bestows benefits on the child. The other child is selectively blind, deaf, dumb, and suffering from whatever other maladies are necessary to make it plausible that he does not even know he has a father. Now either there are some benefits that the father will never bestow unless and until he is asked; and in that case he will do less for his defective child, who surely has more need of his help than does the healthy child. Or, on the other hand, he will bestow all his benefits unasked on the defective child, and then he seems to make a mockery of his practice with the normal child of bestowing some benefits only in response to requests—he is, after all, willing to bestow the same benefits without being asked. So it seems that we are still left with the problem we started with: either God is not perfectly good or the practice of petitionary prayer is pointless. But suppose the father always meets the defective child's needs and desires even though the child never comes to know of the existence of his father. The child knows only that he is always taken care of, and when he needs something, he gets what he needs. It seems to me intuitively clear that such a practice runs a great risk, at least, of making the defective child willful and tyrannical. But even if the defective child is not in danger of being made worse in some respects in this situation, still it seems plain that he would be better off if the father could manage to put the child in a position to know his father and to frame a request for what he wants. So I think a good father will fulfill the child's needs unasked; but I think that he can do so without making a mockery of his practice of bestowing benefits in response to requests only if putting the child in a position to make requests is among his first concerns.

And as for the question whether God would have saved Augustine without Monica's prayers, I think that there is intermediate ground between the assertion that Monica's prayers are necessary to Augustine's salvation, which seems to impugn God's goodness, and the claim that they are altogether without effect, which undercuts petitionary prayer. It is possible, for example, to argue that God would have saved Augustine without Monica's prayers but not in the same amount of time or not by the same process or not with the same effect. Augustine, for instance, might have been converted to Christianity but not in such a way as to become one of its most powerful authorities for centuries.[10]

With all this, I have still looked only at cases that are easy for my position; when we turn to something like a prayer for Guatemala after the earthquake—which begins to come closer to the sort of petitions in the first half of the Lord's Prayer—it is much harder to know what to say. And perhaps it is simply too hard to come up with a reasonable solution here because we need more work on the problem of evil. Why would a good God permit the occurrence of earthquakes in the first place? Do the reasons for his permitting the earthquake affect his afterwards helping the country involved? Our inclination is surely to say that a good God must *in any case* help the earthquake victims, so that in this instance at any rate it is pointless to pray. But plainly we also have strong inclinations to say that a good God must in any case prevent earthquakes in populated areas. And since orthodox Christianity is committed to distrusting these latter inclinations, it is at least at sea about the former ones. Without more work on the problem of evil, it is hard to know what to say about the difference prayer might make in this sort of case.

I think it is worth noticing, though, that the first three requests of the Lord's Prayer do not run into the same difficulties. Those requests seem generally equivalent to a request for the kingdom of God on earth, that state of affairs in which, of their own free will, all men on earth are dedicated, righteous lovers of God. Now suppose it is true that God would bring about his kingdom on earth even if an individual Christian such as Jimmy Carter did not pray for it. It does not follow in this case, however, that the prayer in question is pointless and makes no difference. Suppose no one prayed for the advent of God's kingdom on earth or felt a need or desire for those millennial times strongly enough to pray for them. It seems unreasonable to think that God could bring about his earthly kingdom under those conditions, or if he could, that it would be the state of affairs just described, in which earth is populated by people who *freely* love God. And if so, then making the requests in the first half of the Lord's Prayer resembles other, more ordinary activities in which only the effort of a whole group is sufficient to achieve the desired result. One man can't put out a forest fire, but if everyone in the vicinity of a forest fire realized that fact and on that basis decided not to try, the fire would rage out of control. So in the case of the opening petitions of the Lord's Prayer, too, it seems possible to justify petitionary prayer without impugning God's goodness. Obviously, the account I have given is just a preliminary sketch for the full development of this solution, and a good deal more work needs to be done on the problem. Nonetheless, I think that this account is on the right track and that there is a workable solution to the problem of petitionary prayer which can be summarized in this way. God must work through the intermediary of prayer, rather than doing everything on his own initiative, for man's sake. Prayer acts as a kind of buffer between man and God. By safeguarding the weaker member of the relation from the dangers of overwhelming domination and overwhelming spoiling, it helps to promote and preserve a close relationship between an omniscient, omnipotent, perfectly good person and a fallible, finite, imperfect person. There is, of course, something counter-intuitive in this notion that prayer acts as a buffer; prayer of all sorts is commonly and I think correctly said to have as one of its main functions the production of closeness between man and God. But not just any sort of closeness will result in friendship, and promoting the appropriate sort of closeness will require inhibiting or preventing inappropriate sorts of closeness, so that a relationship of friendship depends on the maintenance of both closeness and distance between the two friends. And while I do not mean to denigrate the importance of prayer in producing and preserving the appropriate sort of closeness, I think the problem of petitionary prayer at issue here is best solved by focusing on the distance necessary for friendship and the function of petitionary prayer in maintaining that distance. . . .

It should be plain that there is nothing in this analysis of prayer which *requires* that God fulfil every prayer; asking God for something is not in itself a sufficient condition for God's doing what he is asked. Christian writings are full of examples of prayers which are not answered, and there are painful cases of unanswered prayer in which the one praying must be tempted more to the belief that God is his implacable enemy than to the sentimental-seeming belief that God is his friend. This paper proposes no answer for these difficulties. They require a long, hard, careful look at the problem of evil, and that falls just outside the scope of this paper.

And, finally, it may occur to someone to wonder whether the picture of God presented in this analysis is at all faithful to the God of the Old or New Testaments. Is this understanding of God and prayer anything that Christianity ought to accept or even find congenial? It seems to me that one could point to many stories in either the Old or New Testament in support of an affirmative answer—for example, Elijah's performance on Mt. Carmel (I Kings 18), or the apostles' prayer for a successor to Judas (Acts 1:24–26). But for a small and particularly nice piece of evidence, we can turn to the story in the Gospel of Luke which describes Jesus making the Lord's Prayer and giving a lecture on how one is to pray. According to the Gospel, Jesus is praying and in such a way that his disciples see him and know that he is praying. One of them makes a request of him which has just a touch of rebuke in it: teach us to pray, as *John* taught *his* disciples to pray (Lk. 11:1). If there is a note of rebuke there, it seems just. A religious master should teach his disciples to pray, and a good teacher does not wait until he is asked to teach his students important lessons. But Jesus is portrayed as a good teacher of just this sort in the Gospel of Luke.[11] Does the Gospel, then, mean its readers to understand that Jesus would not have taught his disciples how to pray if they had not requested it? And if it does not, why is Jesus portrayed as waiting until he is asked? Perhaps the Gospel means us to understand[12] that Jesus does so just in order to teach by experience as well as by sermon what is implicit throughout the Lord's Prayer: that asking makes a difference.

Notes

1. *Cf.*, for example, the similar understanding of this petition in two very different theologians: Augustine, *Homilies on the Gospels,* Serm. 6; and Calvin, *Institutes of the Christian Religion,* III. xx. 41.

2. The most common Old Testament word for "holy" and its correlates is some form of "kādash," the basic, literal meaning of which is separation, withdrawal, or state of being set apart; *cf.* Gesenius, *A Hebrew and English Lexicon of the Old Testament.* In the New Testament, the most frequently used word is *"hagiazō"* and its correlates, the basic meaning of which also includes the notion of being separate and being set apart; *cf.* Thayer, *A Greek–English Lexicon of the New Testament,* and Arndt and Gringrich, *A Greek–English Lexicon of the New Testament and Other Early Christian Literature.*

3. *Cf., e.g.,* Is. 2:2–21, 45:23, and 65:23; Matt. 24; Mk. 13; Lk. 21; and Rev. 6:15–17.

4. See, for example, Martin Luther, *Large Catechism* pt. III. 169. Luther's argument for prayer has more force in the context of the catechism than it does in the context of a philosophical discussion, because Luther's purpose there is the practical one of blocking what he understands as believers' *excuses* for not praying.

5. See reply, a.2.

6. *Cf., e.g.,* Origen, *op. cit.,* and Augustine, *City of God,* Bk. V, ix.

7. See especially Jn. 15:12–15.

8. I want to avoid detailed discussion of the various controversies over omnipotence. For present purposes, I will take this as a rough definition of omnipotence: a being is omnipotent if and only if he can do anything which it is not logically impossible for him to do and if he can avoid doing anything which it is not logically necessary for him to do.

9. Controversy over this point is related to the more general controversy over whether or not it is possible for an omnipotent, omniscient, perfectly good God to create men who would on every occasion freely do what is right. For a discussion of that general controversy and arguments that it is not possible for God to do so, see Alvin Plantinga's *God and Other Minds* (Ithaca, 1967), pp. 132–148; I am in agreement with the general tenor of Plantinga's remarks in that section of his book.

10. I have presented the case of Monica and Augustine in a simplified form in order to have an uncomplicated hard case for the view I am arguing. As far as the historical figures themselves are concerned, it is plain that Monica's overt, explicit, passionate concern for her son's conversion greatly influenced the course of his life and shaped his character from boyhood on. It is not clear whether Augustine would have been anything like the man he was if his mother had not been as zealous on behalf of his soul as she was, if she had not prayed continually and fervently for his salvation and let him know she was doing so. Augustine's character and personality were what they were in large part as a result of her fierce desire for his espousal of Christianity; and just his knowledge that his beloved mother prayed so earnestly for his conversion must have been a powerful natural force helping to effect that conversion. In this context the question whether God could have saved Augustine without Monica's prayers takes on different meaning, and an affirmative answer is much harder to give with reasoned confidence.

11. See, for example, the lessons taught in the two incidents described in Lk. 21:1–6.

12. I have used awkward circumlocutions in this paragraph in order to make plain that it is not my intention here to make any claims about the historical Jesus or the intentions of the Gospel writer. I am not concerned in this paper to do or to take account of contemporary theories of Biblical exegesis. My point is only that the story in the Gospel, as it has been part of ordinary Christian tradition, lends itself to the interpretation I suggest.

❈

WHOM DOES GOD CONSIGN TO HELL?

Stephen T. Davis

Christianity traditionally teaches that at least some people, after death, live eternally apart from God. Let us call those who believe this doctrine *separationists,* because they hold that these people are eternally separated both from God and from the people who are with God. Some Christians, on the other hand, espouse the quite different doctrine known as *universalism.*[1] Universalists believe that all all human beings will ultimately live eternally with God, i.e., that no one will be eternally condemned. . . .

Though I am sympathetic with the intentions of those who espouse universalism, I am not a universalist myself, and will argue against the doctrine in this paper. What I will do here is: (1) state the strongest doctrine of universalism. . . ; (2) present the strongest arguments in favor of it. . . ; (3) reply to these arguments from a separationist standpoint; and (4) make a case for separationism. . . .

Let me now sketch what I take to be a strong doctrine of universalism: God does indeed hate sin and does indeed judge sinners. But God's judgment is always therapeutic; it is designed to bring people to repentance. Thus God's wrath is an integral part of God's loving strategy for reconciling people to God. Some are reconciled to God in this life; some die unreconciled. But God continues to love even those who die apart from God, and to work for their reconciliation. If there is a hell, it exists only for a time, i.e., until the last recalcitrant sinner decides to say yes to God. It is *possible* that hell will exist forever because it is possible some will deny God forever. But after death, God has unlimited time, arguments, and resources to convince people to repent. God will not force anyone into the kingdom; the freedom of God's creatures is always respected. But because of the winsomeness of God's love, we can be sure that God will emerge victorious and that all persons will eventually be reconciled to God. We are all sinners and deserve punishment, but God's love is so great and God's grace so attractive that eventually all persons will be reconciled to God. This, then, is what I take to be a strong version of universalism. Now, what about the arguments in favor? Let me mention five of them.

1. *The Bible implies that universalism is true.* Many universalists are quite prepared to admit that their doctrine is not taught in the Bible and indeed that separationism seems much more clearly taught. Nevertheless, they do typically argue that universalism is at least implied or suggested in various texts. First, it can be pointed out that many texts show that it is God's intention that everyone be reconciled to God. Second, it can be shown that the work of God's grace in Christ was designed for the salvation of everyone. Third, texts can be cited in which God's total victory is proclaimed and in which it is said that everything will ultimately be reconciled to God. Finally, there are texts which seem to the universalists explicitly to predict that all will eventually be reconciled to God.[2] . . .

2. *How can God's purposes be frustrated?* Universalists sometimes argue as follows: eternal sin and eternal punishment would obviously frustrate God's intention that no one be eternally lost. But if God is truly sovereign, how can any divine intention be frustrated? If separationism is true, some will eternally resist God and it follows that god is at least a partial fail-

ure. Surely if God is omnipotent nothing can eternally frustrate the divine aims; if it is God's aim that all be rescued, all *will* be rescued.[3]

3. *How can a just God condemn people to eternal torment?* Universalists frequently argue that no one deserves *eternal* punishment. Perhaps terrible sinners deserve to suffer terribly for a terribly long time. But surely sin should be punished according to its gravity; why do they deserve to suffer for an *infinitely* long time? They certainly do not cause anyone else (or even God) *eternal* sorrow or pain. Suppose we decide that some tyrant, say Nero, deserved to suffer a year in hell for every person he ever killed, injured, treated unfairly, insulted, or even inconvenienced. Suppose further that on this criterion he deserved to suffer for 20,000 years. The problem, however, is that once he has served this sentence he will not have made even the slightest dent in eternity. According to separationism, he must suffer forever. Is this just? It does not seem so. (And this is not even to speak of more run-of-the-mill sinners who perhaps never cause anyone serious harm.)

4. *How can the Blessed experience joy in heaven if friends and loved ones are in hell?* Obviously (so universalists will argue), they can't. People can only know joy and happiness in heaven if everyone else is or eventually will be there too. If the Blessed are to experience joy in heaven, as Christian tradition says they are, universalism must be true.

5. *What about the fate of those who die in ignorance of Christ?* Christianity has traditionally taught that salvation is to be found only in Christ. Jesus is reported as having claimed this very thing: "I am the way, and the truth, and the life; No one comes to the Father but by me" (John 14:6). And this claim seems to dovetail well with standard Christian notions about sin and salvation: there is nothing we can do to save ourselves; all our efforts at self-improvement fail; all we can do is trust in God as revealed in Christ; those who do not know God as revealed in Christ are condemned. And surely—so universalists

argue—the traditional notion is unfair. It is not right to condemn to hell those who die in ignorance of Christ.

Suppose there was a woman named Oohku who lived from
370–320 b.c. in the interior of Borneo. Obviously, she never
heard of Jesus Christ or the Judeo-Christian God; she was
never baptized, nor did she ever make any institutional or psychological commitment to Christ or to the Christian church
She *couldn't* have done these things; she was simply born in the
wrong place and at the wrong time. Is it right for God to condemn this woman to eternal hell just because she was never
able to come to God through Christ? Of course not. The only
way Oohku can be treated fairly by God is if universalism is
true. God is just and loving; thus, universalism is true.

These are the best arguments for universalism that I can
think of. We now need to see how separationists will handle
them and defend their own doctrine.

Let us begin with the biblical argument of the universalist.
The first thing to notice is that separationists like me do not
deny that God desires the salvation of all persons and that
Christ's atoning work was designed to rescue everyone. Accordingly, the texts that emphasize God's total victory and
which seem to universalists to predict universal salvation, the
separationist replies that this is not their proper interpretation.
To affirm that God is ultimately victorious over all enemies
and that God's authority will one day be universally recognized is one thing, and will be agreed on by all Christians. But
to say that every person will eventually be reconciled to God
is quite another, and can only be based on a surprisingly literalistic interpretation of such terms as "all," "all things," "every
knee," and "the world" in the passages cited. It is odd that universalists, who typically protest against literalistic interpretations of the many texts that seem to teach separationism (see
below), appear themselves to adopt a kind of literalism here.
They need to approach the passages cited with a bit more
hermeneutical subtlety; they need to ask (especially in the light

of other texts—again, see below) whether this is what these passages really mean.

Furthermore, the fact that these "universalistic passages" appear in many of the same texts in which separationism seems clearly taught ought make us doubt that universalists interpret them correctly. . . .

Furthermore, separationists can produce a biblical argument of their own, one which is much more compelling. For the reality of hell—and even of eternal hell[4]—*is* spoken of often in the New Testament, and seems inextricably tied to such major themes in New Testament theology as God, sin, judgment, atonement, and reconciliation. Thus it would seem that the introduction of universalism would require severe changes at various other points in the traditional Christian scheme of salvation. . . . In fact, if there is no hell it is hard to see, in New Testament terms, why there would be any need for atonement or a savior from sin. . . . Furthermore, it seems methodologically odd for a person both to deny the reality of eternal hell and (because of biblical teaching and Christian tradition) affirm the reality of heaven. For both seem to stand on an equally firm exegetical and traditional foundation. It is clear that for most universalists, exegetical considerations are outweighed by philosophical ones.

My reply to the biblical argument of the universalist, then, is as follows. It is true that when read in a certain way, a few New Testament and especially Pauline texts might lead one toward universalism. But a careful look shows that not even those texts actually imply universalism. Furthermore, biblically oriented Christians believe that problematical passages on any topic are to be interpreted in the light of the testimony of the whole of scripture, and universalism—so I have argued—is inconsistent with that testimony.

Let me confess that I would deeply like universalism to be true. Like all Christians, I would find it wonderfully comforting to believe that all people will be citizens of the kingdom of God, and certain thorny intellectual problems, especially the problem of evil, might be easier to solve if universalism were true.[5] But as a matter of theological method, we cannot affirm a doctrine just because we would like it to be true. The fact is that separationism is taught in the Bible and that the so-called "universalistic passages" do not imply universalism. That is enough for me; that is why I am a separationist. Philosophical and theological arguments over what God should do are outweighed by the teaching of Scripture. God has revealed to us a doctrine of eternal judgment; we had best accept it. That God has not also revealed to us how to reconcile this doctrine with our understanding of God's love creates a theological problem which we must do our best to solve.

I will now briefly sketch the separationist doctrine I believe in and am prepared to defend. It differs from some traditional theological accounts at two points: (1) For exegetical reasons I do not believe people in hell suffer horrible fiery agony; and (2) while I believe hell in some sense can be spoken of as punishment, I do not believe it is a place where God, so to speak, gets even with those who deny God. It is not primarily a place of retribution.

We know little about hell. Much of what the New Testament says is dearly metaphorical or symbolic. For example, the New Testament uses the metaphor of fire to convey the suffering of people in hell. But this need not mean that condemned people actually suffer the pain of burns. Mark 9:48 describes hell as a place where "the worm does not die" and "the fire is not quenched." Why take the second literally and not the first? I would say both are metaphors of the eternality of hell. The parable of the rich man and Lazarus in Luke 16:19–31 has been taken by some interpreters as a picture of the after-life, but this does not seem sensible. It is a parable, i.e., a made-up story designed to convey a certain religious message. Furthermore, it is difficult to imagine that heaven and hell could be separated by a "great chasm" which cannot be crossed but across which communication can take place. There are many biblical metaphors for hell, e.g., everlasting fire, bottomless pit, outer darkness, place of weeping and gnashing of teeth, place of no rest, place where the uttermost farthing must be paid.[6] None, I would argue, is a literal description.

Hell is a place of separation from God. Not a total separation, of course—that would mean hell would not exist. Furthermore, the biblical tradition denies that anything or anyone can ever be totally separated from God. . . . But hell is separation from God as the source of true love, joy, peace, and light. It is not a place of agony, torment, torture, and utter horror (here I am opposing the lurid and even sadistic pictures of hell envisioned by some Christian thinkers). But there is no deep or ultimate joy there and I believe its citizens are largely miserable. To be apart from the source of love, joy, peace, and light is to live miserably.

Why are the damned in hell? I have already ruled out retribution or any notion of God's "getting even" with them.[7] To put it radically, I believe they are in hell because they choose to be in hell; no one is sent to hell against his or her will.[8] Sadly, some people choose to live their lives apart from God, harden their hearts, and will continue to do so after death; some will doubtless do so forever. For such people, living in God's presence might well seem worse than living in God's absence. Allowing them to live forever in hell is simply God's continuing to grant them the freedom that they enjoyed in this life to say yes or no to God. I nevertheless suspect that people in hell are deeply remorseful. Can people both freely choose hell over heaven, knowing they would be unable to endure heaven, but still be full of remorse that they cannot happily choose heaven? I believe this is quite possible.

Is the existence of hell consistent with God's love and power? Yes, it is. Some Christians try to justify the existence of hell by speaking of it as the "natural consequence" of a life of sin.[9] I accept the notion that hell is the natural consequence of a life of sin (and it is in this sense that hell is a punishment). But this in itself does not justify God in sending people to hell, for it does not justify the divinely-ordained laws of natural necessity that make hell sin's natural consequence. I claim, then, that the people who are in hell are there because they freely choose it, i.e., freely choose not to live in God's presence. If so, then hell can be an expression not only of divine justice but of divine love.

I have been replying to the biblical argument of the universalist. Now I must comment on the others.

How can God's purposes be frustrated? I agree that God desires the salvation of everyone; thus separationism implies that at least one of God's desires is not satisfied: some people will be lost. How can this be, if God is sovereign? The answer is that God created us as free agents; God gave us the ability to say yes or no to God. One of the risks God ran in so doing was precisely that God's purposes *would* be frustrated, and this, sadly, is exactly what has happened. God's will is flaunted whenever anyone sins. It is just not true that "God's will is always done." (Otherwise, why did Jesus teach his disciples to pray, "May your will be done on earth as it is in heaven"—as if God's will is not always done on earth?) Furthermore, it seems that sovereignty entails only *the power* to impose one's will, not the actual imposition of it.

How can a just God condemn someone to eternal torment? In the first place, as already noted, I believe the citizens of hell are there because they freely choose to be there; they have hardened their hearts and would be unable to endure heaven. Unless one bows to God and makes the divine will one's own, heaven is too much to bear and one chooses hell. Thus, as I noted, it is not only just but loving that God allows them to live forever in hell. Second, hell may have the effect on many of strengthening their resolve never to repent; sin may voluntarily continue; and if it is right for evil-doers to experience the consequences of the evil deeds they do here and now, this will be true of the evil deeds they do after death. Third, Christians believe their salvation is a matter of grace alone; we deserve to be condemned, but out of love rather than sheer justice God forgives us and reconciles us to God. The notion of grace, then, is at the heart of the Christian good news. God loves us though we are unlovable; God accepts us though we are unacceptable. But the thing to notice here is that if separationism is inconsistent with God's love, i.e., if a loving God cannot condemn anyone to hell, then our salvation (i.e., our rescue from hell) is no longer a matter of grace; it becomes a matter of our justly being freed from a penalty we don't really deserve. In the end, universalism overturns the Christian notion of grace.

How can the Blessed be joyous if friends and loved ones are in hell? I do not know an adequate answer to this question. I expect that if I knew enough about heaven I would know the answer, but I know little about heaven. The problem is perhaps less acute for me than for those separationists who believe hell is a place of permanent torture. If I am right, the Blessed need not worry that loved ones are in agony and are allowed to hope (see below) that God's love can even yet achieve a reconciliation. But there is still the question how, say, a wife can experience joy and happiness in heaven while her beloved husband is in hell. And that is the question I am unable to answer satisfactorily. It would seem to be unjust for God to allow the wrong choices of the damned—i.e., their rejection of God—to ruin the joy of the Blessed, who have chosen to love God. But how God brings it about that the Blessed experience the joy of the presence of God despite the absence of others, I do not know.

What about the fate of those who die in ignorance of Christ? The main point to note here is that the Bible does not speak in any connected or clear way on this question. Biblical Christians must take seriously those exclusivistic sayings of Jesus and the New Testament writers . . . that create for us this problem. As an orthodox Christian, then, I do believe that salvation is to be found only in Christ. If any person at any time in this life or the next is ever reconciled to God, it is because of the saving work of Jesus Christ. His life, death, and resurrection made it possible. If I am somehow to be reconciled to God, if our imaginary friend Oohku is somehow to be reconciled to God, it is only through Christ that it happens.[10]

Some Christians have taken to heart the Bible's exclusivistic sayings and have concluded that people like Oohku must be lost, that their eternal destiny is hell. But this is to confuse the claim that the Bible is authoritative on matters of faith and practice with the claim that the Bible authoritatively tells us everything we might want to know about Christian faith and practice. It doesn't; I believe the Bible tells us enough so that we can read it, be convicted of sin, and learn how to come to God through Christ. But it does not answer all the questions we might want to ask it and it certainly does not say or imply that those who die in ignorance of Christ are lost. The Bible simply does not in any direct or thorough way address itself to the precise issue of the fate of people like Oohku. The Bible tells us what we *need* to know, not all that we might *want* to know.

What then must the separationist say about the fate of those who die in ignorance of Christ? Again, there is no clear or connected teaching in the Bible on this question; what we find are some vague and unformulated hints which can perhaps guide us but which cannot be used to justify a dogmatic position. . . . I am quite convinced that this much is true— God can indeed make us in any way God pleases and we have no authority over God to challenge this decision. But this by itself does not answer the question of the fate of those who die in ignorance of Christ.

I have also heard the following argument in favor of the claim that it is just for God to send the ignorant to hell: "We are *all* sinners and thus we *all* deserve hell. Thus *no one* is sent to hell who does not deserve hell. It is just that God has graciously allowed or elected some sinners to receive the unmerited gift of salvation. Like everyone else, Oohku deserves to go to hell, so she has no reason to complain when she is sent there." But the answer to this argument is that the described scheme is still radically unjust. Surely it is unfair to those who were not chosen to receive God's grace. Suppose I discover that my two sons are both equally guilty of some wrong—say they both trampled some of my wife's beloved roses in the back yard. And suppose I say to one of them: "You are guilty and your punishment is that you will be confined to your room." And suppose I say to the other one: "You are equally guilty, but as a gift of love, I'm going to let you go without punishment." Surely it is obvious on the face of it that I have been unfair. . . .

Is there, then, any way for the problem of the ignorant to be solved in separationist terms? Here are three assumptions that underlie the position I will take: (1) the Bible does not tell us everything we might want to know about God and the divine will; (2) all people who are reconciled to God are reconciled to God through Christ; (3) it would be unfair for God to condemn the ignorant to hell because they do not believe in Christ. These assumptions push me in the direction of a theological conjecture: that there are ways those who are ignorant of Christ can be reconciled to God through Christ. In other words, if redemption is to be found only in Christ, and if the atoning work of Christ was intended for all people, and if God is loving and just, then it seems sensible to suppose that it must be causally possible for all people, wherever or whenever they live or however ignorant they are, to come to God through Christ. (I would like to stress that this is a conjecture, not a dogma or a teaching or even a firm belief.) . . .

As long as it is recognized that these are conjectures without systematic or clear biblical warrant, we might even suggest that Christ has the power to save human beings *wherever* they are, even in hell.[11] I recognize some will resist this suggestion. It is one thing—they will say—to suggest that the ignorant after death receive a chance (their first) to respond positively to the gospel. But it is quite another to suggest that those who have been condemned receive *other* chances to respond positively. But a question must be asked here: Is it possible that there are persons who would respond positively to God's love after death even though they have not responded positively to it before death? I believe this is possible. In fact, one reason for this latest conjecture is the observation that some who hear the gospel hear it in such a way that they are psychologically unable to respond positively. Perhaps they heard the gospel for the first and only time from a fool or a bigot or a scoundrel. Or perhaps they were caused to be prejudiced against Christianity by skeptical parents of teachers. Whatever the reason, I believe it would be unjust of God to condemn those who did indeed hear the good news but were unable to respond positively. This is why I suggest that even in hell, people can be rescued.[12]

Does this bring in universalism by the back door? Certainly not. I have little doubt some will say no to God eternally (the Bible predicts this, in fact), nor do I see any need for a "second chance" for those who have freely and knowingly chosen in this life to live apart from God. Perhaps God never gives up on people, but some folk seem to have hardened their heart to such a degree that they will never repent. For such people, hell as separation from God exists forever, just as it exists for them now. But perhaps some who die in ignorance of Christ will hear the good news, repent, and be rescued. Perhaps even some citizens of hell will do so too. Again, the key word is *perhaps*. We have no ground to dogmatize here. I do not think we *know* the fate of those who die in ignorance of Christ. All I am sure of is that God's scheme for the salvation of human beings will turn out to have been just, perhaps in ways we cannot now understand.

Notes

1. Among recent and contemporary Christians, Nicholas Berdyaev, William Temple, C. H. Dodd, Nels Ferre, William Barclay, J. A. T. Robinson, and John Hick have all defended some form of universalism. Karl Barth has been accused of espousing the doctrine.

2. First point: see Romans 11:32, I Timothy 2:4–6, II Peter 3:9. Second point: II Corinthians 5:14, 15; Titus 2:11; Hebrews 2:9; 1 John 2:2. Third point: see I Corinthians 15:22; cf. 23–28; II Corinthians 5:19; Colossians 1:19. Fourth point: see Romans 5:18; Philippians 2:9–11; John 1:29; 3:17; 12:32, 47.

3. See, for example, J. A. T. Robinson, *In the End, God* (London: James Clarke and Co., 1950), p.107.

4. See Mark 9:43–50; Matthew 25:41, 46; II Thessalonians 1:7–9; Jude 6; Revelation 14:11; 19:3; 20:10.

5. As, above all, John Hick has seen. See *Evil and the God of Love* (London: Macmillan and Co., 1966), pp. 98, 113–120, 183, 377–381.

6. Respectively: Matthew 25:41, Revelation 9:2, Matthew 8:12, Revelation 14:11, Matthew 5:26.

7. It must be admitted that there are New Testament texts that can be taken to imply that hell is an act of vengeance or retribution on sinners. See Matthew 5:22, 29; 8:12; 10:15; II Thessalonians 1:6–9; Hebrew 2:2–3; 10:28–31; II Peter 2:4–9, 12–13. Some even seem to suggest degrees of punishment corresponding to degrees of guilt. See Matthew 11:22–24; Luke 12:47–48; 20:47.

8. "To choose finally and for ever—unfathomable mystery of iniquity—to say 'No' to Jesus is to be held in a hell of one's own choosing and making. It is not God who makes hell, for hell is the contradiction of all that is God." T. F. Torrance, "Universalism or Election?" *Scottish Journal of Theology,* Vol. 2, No. 3 (September, 1949), p. 317.

9. See John Wenham, *The Goodness of God* (Downer's Grove, Illinois: Inter-Varsity Press, 1974), p. 38fn, and P. T. Geach, *Providence and Evil* (Cambridge: Cambridge University Press, 1977), pp. 128, 138–140, 147.

10. As suggested by C. S. Lewis in *The Great Divorce* (New York: The Macmillan Company, 1957), pp. 120–124.

11. A suggestion also perhaps made (in literary form) by C. S. Lewis in *The Great Divorce*.

12. See Revelation 21:25, where the city of God is described as follows: "Its gates shall never be shut by day—and there shall be no night there."

NINE

DOES GOD SUFFER?

Nicholas Wolterstorff

My heart grew sombre with grief, and wherever I looked I saw only death. My own country became a torment and my own home a grotesque abode of misery. All that we had done together was now a grim ordeal without him. My eyes searched everywhere for him, but he was not there to be seen. I hated all the places we had known together, because he was not in them and they could no longer whisper to me, 'Here he comes!' as they would have done had he been alive but absent for a while. . . . My soul was a burden, bruised and bleeding. It was tired of the man who carried it, but I found no place to set it down to rest. (Augustine, Confessions IV, 4; IV, 7)[1]

It is in passages such as this, where he exposes to full view the grief which overwhelmed him upon the death of his dear friend from Tagaste, that Augustine is at his most appealing to us. . . . We are attracted both by the intensity of his love and grief, and by his willingness to expose that grief to his friends and the readers of his *Confessions.* To any who may have experienced torments similar to those Augustine here describes, the passage also has the mysteriously balming quality of expressing with delicate precision the grief they themselves have felt. All the places and all the objects that once whispered "Here he comes" or "Here she comes" have lost their voice and fallen achingly mute.

It is a rough jolt, to discover that at those very points in his life where we find Augustine most appealing, he, from the time of his conversion onward, found himself thoroughly disgusting. His reason for exposing his grief was to share with his readers his confession to God of the senselessness and sinfulness of a love so intense for a being so fragile that its destruction could cause such grief. "Why do I talk of these things?" he asks. And he answers, "It is time to confess, not to question" (*Confessions* IV, 6).

In the years between the death of his friend and the death of his mother Augustine embraced the Christian faith. That embrace made his response to his mother's death very different from that to his friend's. "I closed her eyes," he says,

> and a great wave of sorrow surged into my heart. It would have overflowed in tears if I had not made a strong effort of will and stemmed the flow, so that the tears dried in my eyes. What a terrible struggle it was to hold them back! As she breathed her last, the boy Adeodatus began to wail aloud and only ceased his cries when we all checked him. I, too, felt that I wanted to cry like a child, but a more mature voice within me, the voice of my heart, bade me keep my sobs in check, and I remained silent. (*Confessions* IX, 12)

On that earlier occasion, tears and "tears alone were sweet to him, for in his heart's desire they had taken the place of his friend" (*Confessions* IV, 4). In his reminiscences he asked why that was so, "why tears are sweet to the sorrowful." "How . . . can it be that there is sweetness in the fruit we pluck from the bitter crop of life, in the mourning and the tears, the wailing and the sighs?" (*Confessions* IV, 5). But now, on the occasion of his mother's death, he "fought against the wave of sorrow" (*Confessions* IX, 12).

His struggle for self-control was not successful. He reports that after the burial, as he lay in bed thinking of his mother, "the tears which I had been holding back streamed down, and I let them flow as freely as they would, making of them a pillow for my heart. On them it rested . . ." (*Confessions* IX, 12). So now, he says to God, "I make you my confession. . . . Let any man read it who will. . . . And if he finds that I sinned by weeping for my mother, even if only for a fraction of an hour, let him not mock at me . . . but weep himself, if his charity is great. Let him weep for my sins to you . . ." (*Confessions* IX, 12). The sin for which Augustine wants the person of charity to weep, however, is not so much the sin of weeping over the death of his mother as the sin of which that weeping was a sign. I was, says Augustine, "guilty of too much worldly affection."

Obviously there is a mentality coming to expression here which is profoundly foreign to us. In our own day there are still those who hold back tears—usually because they think it unbecoming to cry, seldom because they think it sinful. But rare is the person who believes that even to *feel* grief upon the death of a friend or one's mother is to have been guilty of too much worldly affection. The mentality expressed not only shapes Augustine's view of the proper place of sorrow and suffering in human life; it also contributes to his conviction that in God there is no sorrow or suffering. God's life is a life free of sorrow—indeed, a life free of upsetting emotions in general, a life free of passions, a life of apathy, untouched by suffering, characterized only by steady bliss. In thus thinking of God, Augustine was by no means alone. Indeed, the view that God's life is that of blissful non-suffering apathy enjoyed near total consensus until the twentieth century. . . .

But why would anyone who placed himself in the Christian tradition think of God's life as that of non-suffering apathy?

The identity of that tradition is determined (in part) by the adherence of its members, in one way or another, to the scriptures of the Old and New Testaments. And even those who read while running cannot fail to notice that God is there pictured as one who sufferingly experiences his world and therefore grieves. What was it, then, that led the tradition to 'bracket' this dimension of the biblical picture of God? . . .

We cannot do better than begin with Augustine. But we would be ill-advised to move at once to what Augustine said about emotions and sufferings in the life of God. For it was true of Augustine, as it was of most others in the tradition, that his reflections on the place of emotions and suffering in God's life were merely a component within his more comprehensive reflections on the place of emotions and suffering in the ideal life of persons generally—divine and human together. We must try, then, to grasp that totality. Let us begin with what Augustine says about the proper place of emotions and suffering in human experience.

Augustine frames his thought within the eudaemonistic tradition of antiquity. We are all in search of happiness—by which Augustine and the other ancients did not mean life in which happiness outweighs grief and ennui but a life from which grief and ennui have been cast out—a life of uninterrupted bliss. Furthermore, Augustine aligns himself with the Platonic tradition in his conviction that one's love, one's *eros*, is the fundamental determinant of one's happiness. Augustine never imagined that a human being could root out *eros* from his existence.[2] Incomplete beings that we are, we inescapably long for fulfillment. The challenge, accordingly, is to choose objects for one's love such that happiness ensues.

Now it was as obvious to Augustine as it is to all of us that grief ensues when that which we love is destroyed or dies, or is altered in such a way that we no longer find it lovable. Says he, in reflecting on his grief upon the death of his friend, "I lived in misery like every man whose soul is tethered by the love of things that cannot last and then is agonized to lose them. . . . The grief I felt for the loss of my friend had struck so easily into my inmost heart simply because I had poured out my soul upon him, like water upon sand, loving a man who was mortal as though he were never to die" (*Confessions* IV, 6; IV, 8). The cure is to detach one's love from such objects and to attach it to something immutable and indestructible. For Augustine, the only candidate was God. "Blessed are those who love you, O God. . . . No one can lose you . . . unless he forsakes you" (*Confessions* IV, 9). . . .

Prominent in the ethical philosophy of middle and late antiquity were discussions over the proper place of emotions in life. In those discussions, the Stoic view was famous. Augustine, in *The City of God*, participates in those discussions by staking out his own position on the proper place of emotions in the life of the godly person in opposition to the Stoic position.

Now the Stoics did not say that in the ideal life there would be no emotional coloring to one's experience. They insisted, on the contrary, that in such a life there would be various non-perturbing emotions which they called *eupatheiai*. They regularly cited three of these: Joy, wishfulness, and caution. Their thought was that the ideal life, the happy life, is the life of the wise person—of the person who, by virtue of directing his life by reason, is a person whose character and intentions are morally virtuous. To make it clear that, in their judgment, the only thing good in itself is moral good, they typically refused even to *call* anything else "good." Certain other things are, at best, *preferable*. The wise person, then, will rejoice over the moral status he has attained, will wish for the continuation of that status, and will be watchful for what threatens it.

The Stoics went on to say, though, that the sage would be without *pathos*, without passion. He would be *apathés*, apathetic. His condition would be that of *apatheia*—apathy, impassibility, passionlessness. What did they mean? . . .

[T]he founding fathers of Stoicism, Zeno and Chrysippus, said that a *pathos* is "an excessive impulse," "a 'disease' which affects our basic impulses," "an irrational movement of the soul," "an unnatural movement of the soul which is contrary to reason," etc. And by such sayings they meant to imply, among other things, that a *pathos* is based on, or is even to be identified with, a judgment which is false and contrary to reason. Passions are based on (or identical with) erroneous judgments of evaluated fact that lead to (or are) irrational feelings and excessive impulses. But if this is one's understanding of a *pathos*, then obviously one will hold that passions will in no form whatsoever appear in the life of the fully wise person. And that in fact is what the mainline Stoics claimed when they said that the wise person will be characterized by *apatheia*.

In principle the question remains open, however, whether all emotional disturbances—with fear, grief, and ecstasy as prime examples—are *passions* on this concept of passion. It is clear that the classic Stoics thought they were. One grieves, they would have said, only over what one evaluates as evil; but the sage, finding no trace of moral evil in himself, has nothing over which to grieve. So too, one fears what one evaluates as an evil threatening; but for the sage, who is steady in virtue, there are no threatening evils. And one goes into ecstasy over something that happens to come one's way which one evaluates as good. But for the sage, there are no goods which just happen to come his way; that which is the only thing good for him, namely, his own moral character, is entirely of his own making. It was, thus, the contention of the classic Stoics that as a matter of fact the upsetting emotions are all passions, and will, on that account, have no place in the life of the wise person. The true sage experiences no emotional disturbances. . . .[3]

We have been speaking of the place of the passion in the life of the imperfectly godly person in this imperfect world of ours. But, we must be reminded that Augustine also points us away from life in this world to a perfected life in a perfected world—a life not earned or achieved but granted. In that life there will be no such emotional disturbances as grief and fear. For that will be a life of uninterrupted bliss; and "who that is affected by fear or grief can be called absolutely blessed?" Even "when these affections are well regulated, and according to God's will, they are peculiar to this life, not to that future life we look for" (*City of God* XIV, 9). Augustine's argument, as we have seen, is not the Stoic argument that the passions are always based on false evaluations; they are not. His argument is that having emotions always involves *being overcome*, and that the pain embedded within such emotions as grief and fear is incompatible with full happiness. Grief and fear are not as such incompatible with *reason*. They are as such incompatible with *eudaemonia*. Hence the abolition of those passions from our lives will not occur by way of illumination as to the true nature of things. It will occur by way of removal from our existence of that which it is appropriate to fear or grieve over.

So our perfected existence will exhibit not only *eros* attached entirely to God, but apathy. For attachment to God and detachment from world, we struggle here and now. For *apathy,* we merely long, in the meanwhile fearing and grieving over the evil worth fearing and grieving over. Struggle and longing, aiming and hoping, pull apart in the Augustinian universe. It is not, though—let it be repeated—a feelingless apathy for which we long. We long for a life of joy and bliss. . . .

And now the eternal life of God, as understood by Augustine, can be very simply described: God's life satisfies the eudaemonistic ideal implicit in all that has preceded. God's life is through and through blissful. Thus God too is free of negative *pathe*. Of *Mitleiden* with those who are suffering, God feels nothing, as also he feels no pain over the shortfall of godliness in his errant creatures. His state is *apatheia*—an *apatheia* characterized positively by the steady non-perturbing state of joy.

God dwells eternally in blissful non-suffering *apatheia*. Nothing that happens in the world alters his blissful unperturbed serenity. Certainly God is not oblivious to the world. There is in him a steady disposition of benevolence toward his human creatures. But this disposition to act benevolently proceeds on its uninterrupted successful course whatever transpires in the world.

In sum, the Augustinian God turns out to be remarkably like the Stoic sage: devoid of passions, unfamiliar with longing, foreign to suffering, dwelling in steady bliss, exhibiting to others only benevolence. . . .

Augustine does indeed make clear that in one important respect God's life is not to be identified with our eudaemonistic ideal. In humanity's perfected existence *eros* is fixed steadily on God. God, in contrast, has no *eros*. Since there is in him no lack, he does not reach out to what would fulfill him. God reaches out exclusively in the mode of benevolence, not in the mode of *eros*. . . .

Are we to say, then, that in his picture of God as dwelling in blissful non-suffering apathy Augustine shows that, whatever be the qualifications he wishes to make for human beings, he still embraces the late antique, Stoic notion of what constitutes perfect existence? Is that the bottom line? Yes, I think we must indeed say this—not only for Augustine but for the tradition in general. Shaped as they were by the philosophical traditions of late antiquity, it was inconceivable to the church fathers that God's existence should be anything other than perfect and that ideal existence should be anything other than blissful. . . .

It is possible, however, to be struck by quite a different aspect of the picture; namely, God remains blissfully unperturbed while humanity drowns in misery. When looked at in this way the picture's look is startlingly reversed, from the compelling to the grotesque. It is this grotesque look of the picture which has forcefully been called to our attention by various contemporary thinkers as they have launched an attack on the traditional picture of the apathetic God. . . .

Far and away the most commonly used argument in the contemporary discussion is that if God truly loves his suffering children, then he himself will feel their misery with them. God's love must include that mode of love which is sympathy, *Mitleiden*. Perhaps the most vivid statement of this argument was composed by an English writer, Maldwyn Hughes, early in the century in his book, *What is Atonement? A Study in the Passion of Christ.* Hughes says:

> We must choose whether or not we will accept the Christian revelation that 'God is love.' If we do, then we must accept the implication of the revelation. . . . It is an entire misuse of words to call God our loving Father, if He is able to view the waywardness and revelation of His children without being moved by grief and pity. . . . It is of the very nature of love to suffer when its object suffers loss, whether inflicted by itself or others. If the suffering of God be denied, then Christianity must discover a new terminology and must obliterate the statement 'God is love' from its Scriptures.[4]

It is clear that between this view of the life of God and the Augustinian view there is a deep clash of ideals: The ideal divine life for Augustine was that of uninterrupted suffering-free bliss; the ideal divine life for the moderns is a life of sympathetic love. In effect the moderns insist that the solidarity of grieving and rejoicing which Augustine recommends for humanity on this earth is to embrace God as well. How can we adjudicate between these profoundly different visions?

Little will be gained by the moderns' simply citing biblical passages about God as loving. For Augustine and the other church fathers who defended the non-suffering apathy of God had not overlooked the fact that the Bible speaks of God loving. And they too were committed to the teachings of the prophets and apostles. It was their conviction, however, that all the statements about God's love could be, and should be, interpreted in a manner consistent with God's apathy and his freedom from suffering.

Augustine's proposal became classic.[5] Scripture everywhere witnesses that God is pitiful, he says. But the pity of God differs from human pity. Human pity brings "misery of heart"; whereas "who can sanely say that God is touched by any misery?" "With regard to pity, if you take away the compassion which involves a sharing of misery with whom you pity, so that there remains the peaceful goodness of helping and freeing from misery, some kind of knowledge of the divine pity is suggested."[6] In short: The love that we are to attribute to God is not the love and sympathy, of *Mitleiden*, in which one shares the feelings of the other; it is the love of well-doing, of benevolence, of agape.

And in general, as to the predication of the language of the emotions to God: this must all be interpreted as attributing to God those *effects* of his agency which are similar to the effects of the perturbing emotions in us:

> God's repentance does not follow upon error, the anger of God carries with it no trace of a disturbed mind, nor his pity the wretched heart of a fellow-sufferer, . . . nor His jealousy and envy of mind. But by the repentance of God is meant the change of things which lie within His power, unexpected by man; the anger of God is His vengeance upon sin; the pity of God is the goodness of His help; the jealousy of God is that providence whereby He does not allow those whom He has in subjection to Himself to love with impunity what He forbids.[7]

The conclusion is that "when God repents He is not changed but He brings about change; when He is angry He is not moved but He avenges; when He pities He does not grieve but He liberates; when He is jealous He is not pained but He causes pain."[8]

So it is clear that the classical tradition of the apathetic God will not come crashing down simply by observing that the Scriptures speak of God as loving and then adding that if God loves his suffering human creatures, he must himself suffer. The tradition interpreted the biblical passages in question as speaking of God's non-suffering benevolence. We seem to be at an impasse.

Perhaps some advance can be made if we pause to reflect a bit on the nature of the emotions; for these, after all, are central in the discussion. Let me here make use of the results of some probing discussions on the nature of emotion to be found in the philosophical literature of the past fifteen years or so, results skillfully pulled together and amplified by William Lyons in his recent book, *Emotion*.[9] The upshot of the philosophical discussions is decisively in favor of the so-called *cognitive* theory of emotion—a theory already prominent, in its essentials, among the ancients and the medievals.

The cognitive theory holds, in the first place, that every episode of emotion incorporates a *belief* that such and such a state of affairs has occurred or is occurring or may well occur, along with an *evaluation* of that state of affairs (proposition). Every emotion has, in that way, a doxastic/evaluative component, and thereby a propositional content. Of course the belief which the emotion incorporates may well be mistaken: Emotions may be either veridical or non-veridical. Suppose, for example (to take one of Lyons' illustrations) that I am afraid that the large dog approaching will attack me. The proposition (state of affairs) that the large dog will attack me is then the propositional content of the emotion; and a central component of the emotion will be my believing and evaluating, be it negatively or positively, that state of affairs.

The reference to evaluation is important and must not be lost from view. The propositional content of an emotion is not only believed but evaluated. If I were indifferent to being attacked by the large dog, rather than evaluating such an attack with distinct negativity, I would feel no emotion in that regard. Or if I evaluated this state of affairs positively, out of exhibitionism or a desire for martyrdom, I would feel not fear but exhiliration.

The propositional content of an emotion along with one's negative or positive evaluation of that content, plays a central role in the identification of an emotion. But it is not the whole of the emotion. There is no emotion unless the belief and evaluation cause a physiological disturbance in the person (the sympathetic nervous system being central here), along with certain characteristic feelings which are, in part, awareness of one's physiological disturbance. What proves to be the case is that the physiological disturbance and the accompanying feelings differ remarkably little from one kind of emotion to another. One cannot, for example, differentiate anger from fear on this basis.

Lastly, many if not all emotions incorporate a characteristic appetitive component—a desire to do something or other so as, for example, to eliminate the state of affairs in question or to continue it, etc. The person afraid that the large approaching dog will attack him is strongly desirous of doing something to avert the attack—though it may happen that his physiological disturbance becomes so severe that, instead of running like a gazelle so as to implement his desire to avoid attack, he sinks down helpless as a jellyfish. It is the appetitive component in emotions that accounts for the fact that emotions can function as motives for intentionally undertaken actions: a person may run away *out* of fear, may send a blistering letter *out of* anger, etc.

Now if this schematic analysis of the nature of emotions is correct in its main outlines, it follows directly that God has no emotions: No grief, no anger, no fear, and so forth. For a person can have an emotion only if that person is capable of being physiologically upset. And God, having no physiology, is not so capable. . . . In the sense of *pathos* which we have been using in our discussion, we can conclude that God is lacking in *pathos*. The tradition was right: God is apathetic. He does not grieve, neither in sympathy nor, as it were, on his own.

But we must not conclude from this that the contest is over and that the ancients are victorious in their combat with the moderns. For though the issue of whether God suffers is regularly blurred with the issue of whether God has passions, I suggest that suffering is in fact a distinct phenomenon from grief and the other 'negative' emotion, and that the conclusion that God has no passions still leaves open the question whether God suffers. It remains an open question whether God's apathy is a *suffering* apathy.

A person grieving over some loss is suffering. It will be recalled that the recognition that grief has a component of suffering is what led Augustine to conclude that God does not experience the passion of grief. But human suffering is by no means confined to emotional states. There is also the suffering caused by physical pain, the suffering caused by mental depression, the suffering caused by the desperate wish that one's sexual orientation were different from what it is, and so forth. Furthermore, it is often the case that even when the emotional state of grief subsides, the suffering continues.

What then are the connections among the belief that some loss has occurred, the emotional state of grieving over that loss, and the suffering comprised in that grieving? Well, clearly the cause of the suffering that one experiences in grieving is not the physiological disturbance or the accompanying feelings. These are not to be thought of as one of the sources of suffering in our existence, on a par with physical pain and mental depression. For as we have seen, the actual feelings involved in grief are little different from those in great joy. There are tears of joy as well as tears of grief. And it is worth recalling Augustine's observation that the grieving person may even find sweetness in the tears of his grief.

One is tempted to conclude, then, that the cause of the suffering that one experiences when grieving is the event over which one is grieving: the death, the maiming, the defeat, whatever. But this too cannot be correct. For there may be no such event! One may *believe* that the death, the maiming, the defeat, occurred when it did not. There may in fact be no event such that one grieves over it and it caused one's grief. And conversely, if some event occurred but one does not believe it did, the event causes no grief.

The conclusion must be, I think, that the cause of one's suffering, when grieving over loss, is simply *one's believing* that a loss occurred. For whether or not a loss of the sort in question occurred, the *believing* definitely exists. When someone suffers from physical pain, eliminating the pain eliminates the suffering. When someone suffers over mental depression, getting rid of the depression gets rid of the suffering. So too, the suffering one experiences when grieving over loss is eliminated by elimination of the belief that the loss occurred. When the prodigal son, thought to be dead, returns home alive, the father's tears of grief are transmitted into tears of joy. Physical pain and mental depression and unsatisfied desire cause suffering. But so also do certain of our ways of representing reality. And it makes no difference whether those ways be faithful to reality or unfaithful—veridical or non-veridical.

We speak naturally of the suffering *caused* by pain, of the suffering *caused* by mental depression, etc. But we must not think of the connection between some facet of our experience, on the one hand, and joy or suffering, on the other, as the connection of efficient causality. The suffering *caused* by pain is not some distinct sensation caused by the pain sensation. Suffering and joy are, as it were, adverbial modifiers of the states and events of consciousness. Pain and depression and the belief that someone we love has died are episodes of consciousness that occur sufferingly. The experience of art and the taste of good food and the belief that one of our projects has succeeded are episodes of consciousness that occur joyfully. A fundamental fact of consciousness is that events of consciousness do not all occur indifferently. Some occur unpleasantly, on a continuum all the way to suffering; some occur pleasantly, on a continuum all the way to joy; and some, indeed, occur in neither mode.

Suffering, when veridical, is an existential No-saying to something in reality. With one's very existence one says "No" to the pain, "No" to the mental depression. But when that state of consciousness which causes the grief is one which has a propositional content, then that to which one existentially says "No" pulls apart from the cause of the suffering. One existentially says "No" to the loss, not to the believing; "No" to the desire's being unfulfilled, not to the desiring. (The suffering may of course lead one to say "No" to the desire itself.)

Earlier we spoke of emotions as including an evaluative component. But quite clearly there is no emotion if we just coolly evaluate something as meeting or not meeting some criterion that we happen to embrace. The evaluation must be an existential *valuing* of which we have just now been speaking. At the core of an emotion will be our *valuing* of the facts and supposed facts of the world. And that valuing may continue even though the emotion subsides.

One more observation is relevant: The fact that suffering consists of the (intensely) aversive occurrence of some state or event of consciousness in compatible with the fact that often we choose to do what we anticipate will cause us suffering. We choose the surgery knowing that pain will follow. In this there is nothing complex or mysterious. To understand it, we need only remind ourselves that, as means to achieving what one desires, one may do that which (as such) one does not desire. Truly mysterious, however, is the fact that one may get *joy out of suffering*—as, for example, the person of intense religiosity who shares in the suffering of Christ and 'counts it all joy'. In such a case, the person joyfully experiences his sufferingly experiencing pain. . . .

Does God sufferingly experience what transpires in the world? The tradition said that he does not. The moderns say that he does—specifically, that he sufferingly experiences our suffering. Both parties agree that God loves the world. But the tradition held that God loves only in the mode of benevolence; it proposed construing all the biblical passages in the light of that conviction.[10] The moderns insist that God's love includes love in the mode of sympathy. The moderns paint in attractive colors a moral ideal which is an alternative to that of the tradition, and point to various biblical passages speaking of God's suffering love—passages which the tradition, for centuries, has construed in its own way. The tradition, for its part, offered essentially two lines of defense. It argued that the attribution of emotion and suffering to God was incompatible with God's unconditionedness, an argument which, so we have concluded, should be rejected. And second, it offered a pair of what it took to be obvious truths: that suffering is incompatible with ideal existence, and that God's existence is immutably ideal. We saw that the supposition that those truths are obvious was endangered in Augustine's case by his insistence that we human beings are to cultivate a solidarity of grieving over evil and rejoicing over repentance. But we did not ourselves offer any argument directly against those supposed truths.

How can we advance from here? Perhaps by looking more intently than we have thus far at that claim of the tradition that God's love consists exclusively of benevolence. Benevolence in God was understood as his steady disposition to do good to his creatures. And since as long as there are creatures—no matter what their condition—there is scope for God's exercise of that disposition, and since his exercise of that disposition is never frustrated, God endlessly takes joy in this dimension of himself. He does not take joy—let us carefully note—in his awareness of the condition of his creatures. He does not delight in beholding the creaturely good that he has brought about. If that were the case, his joy would be conditional on the state of things other than himself. What God joyfully experiences is simply his own exercise of benevolence. God's awareness of our plunge into sin and suffering causes him no disturbance; his awareness of the arrival of his perfected kingdom will likewise give him no joy. For no matter what the state of the world, there is room for God's successful exercise of his steady disposition to do good; and it is in *that* exercise that he finds delight.

An analogue which comes to mind is that of a professional health-care specialist. Perhaps when first she entered her profession she was disturbed by the pain and limping and death she saw. But that is now over. Now she is neither perturbed nor delighted by the condition of the people that she sees. What gives her delight is just her inner awareness of her own well-doing. And always she finds scope for well-doing—so long, of course, as she has clients. To those who are healthy she gives reassuring advice on health maintenance. To those who are ill she dispenses medicine and surgery. But it makes no differences to her whether or not her advice maintains the health of the healthy and whether or not her proffered concoctions and cuttings cure the illness of the ill. What makes a difference is just her steadiness in well-doing; in this and in this alone she finds her delight. If it falls within her competence she will, of course, cooperate in pursuing the elimination of smallpox; that is doing good. But should the news arrive of its elimination, she will not join the party; she has all along been celebrating the only thing she finds worth celebrating—namely, her own well-doing. She is a Stoic sage in the modern world.

I dare say that most of us find such a person thoroughly repugnant; that shows how far we are from the mentality of many of the intellectuals in the world of late antiquity. But beyond giving vent to our feelings of repugnance, let us consider whether the picture I have drawn is even coherent. Though this person neither rejoices nor suffers over anything in the condition of her patients, nonetheless she rejoices in her own doing of good. But what then does she take as *good*? What does she *value*? The health of her patients, one would suppose. Why otherwise would she give advice to the one on how to maintain his health, and chemicals to the other to recover his, and all the while rejoice, on account of thus acting, in her own doing of good? But if she does indeed value the health of her patients, then perforce she will also be glad over its presence and disturbed by its absence (when she knows about these). Yet we have pictured her as neither happy nor disturbed by anything other than her own well-doing. Have we not described what cannot be?

Perhaps in his description of moral action that great Stoic philosopher of the modern world, Immanuel Kant, can be of help to us here. In the moral dimension of our existence, the only thing good in itself is a good will, said Kant. Yet, of course, the moral person will do such things as act to advance the health of others. Insofar as she acts morally, however, she does not do so because her awareness of health in people gives her delight and her awareness of illness proves disturbing. She may indeed be so constituted that she does thus value health and sickness in others and act thereon. But that is no moral credit to her. To be moral she must act not out of delight over health nor out of disturbance over illness but out of duty. She must act on some rule specifying what one ought to do in her sort of situation—a rule to which, by following, she accords 'respect'. That is what it is to value good will: to act out of respect for the moral law rather than out of one's natural likings and dislikings, rejoicings and grievings. And the moral person is the person who, wherever relevant, thus values the goodness of her will. Her valuing of that will mean, when her will is in fact good, that she will delight therein. But if she acts out of a desire to delight in having a good will, that too is not moral action; she must act out of respect for the moral law.

Suppose then that our health-care specialist values the goodness of her will and acts thereon by dutifully seeking to advance the health of her patients—delighting in thus acting. She may or may not also value the health of her patients, being disturbed by its absence and delighted by its presence. But if she does not in that way value her patients' health, that does not in any way militate against her delighting in her own well-doing.

We have here, then, a way of understanding how it can be that God delights in his doing good to human beings without either delighting in, or being disturbed by, the human condition. God acts out of duty. Thus acting, he values his own good will without valuing anything in his creation. If we interpret God's benevolence as his acting out of duty, then the traditional picture becomes coherent.

But of course it buys this coherence at great price. For to think thus of God is to produce conflict at a very deep level indeed with the Christian scriptures. These tell us that it is not out of duty but out of love that God blesses us, not out of obligation but out of grace that he delivers us. To construe God's love as purely benevolence and to construe his benevolence along Kantian-Stoic lines as his acting out of duty, is to be left without God's love.

So we are back with the model in which God values things other than his own good will—values positively some of the events and conditions in his creation, and values negatively others. To act out of love toward something other than oneself is to value that thing and certain states of that thing. And on this point it matters not whether the love be erotic or agapic. If one rejects the duty-model of God's action, then the biblical speech about God's prizing of justice and shalom in his creation will have to be taken at face value and not construed as meaning that God has a duty to work for justice and shalom. . . .

I come then to this conclusion: the fact that the biblical writers speak of God as rejoicing and suffering over the state of the creation is not a superficial eliminable feature of their speech. It expresses themes deeply embedded in the biblical vision. God's love for his world is a rejoicing and suffering love. The picture of God as a Stoic sage, ever blissful and non-suffering, is in deep conflict with the biblical picture.[11]

But are we entitled to say that it is a *suffering* love, someone may ask—a love prompted by a *suffering* awareness of what goes on in the world. An unhappy awareness, Yes; but does it reach all the way to suffering?

What the Christian story says is that God the Father, out of love for humanity, delivered his only begotten Son to the suffering and abandonment and death of the cross. In light of that, I think it grotesque to suggest that God's valuing of our human predicament was so mildly negative as to cause him no suffering. But in any case, nothing of importance hangs on degrees. The claim of the tradition was that God's knowledge of the world gives him no vexation *at all*, no disturbance, no unhappiness. We have seen reason to think that that claim is false.

In closing let me observe that if we agree that God both sufferingly and joyfully experiences this world of ours and of his, then at once there comes to mind a question which the tradition never asked; namely, What in our world causes God suffering and what in it causes him joy? And then at once there also comes to mind a vision of the relation between *our* suffering and joy and *God's* suffering and joy which is profoundly different from that to be found in the tradition. In the tradition the relation was simply that here in this life we long to share in that uninterrupted bliss which God from eternity enjoys. What now comes to mind instead is the vision of *aligning ourselves* with God's suffering and with his joy: of delighting over that which is such that his awareness of our delight gives him delight and of suffering over that which is such that his awareness of our suffering causes him suffering. . . .

To some of the things in this world one can pay the tribute of recognizing in them worth sufficient to merit a love which plunges one into suffering upon their destruction. In one's love one can say a "Yes" to the worth of persons or things and in one's suffering a "No" to their destruction. To friends and relatives one can pay the tribute of loving them enough to suffer upon their death. To justice among one's people one can pay the tribute of loving it enough to suffer upon its tyrannical denial. To the delights of music and voice and birdsong one can pay the tribute of loving them enough to suffer upon going deaf. One can pay to persons and things the existential tribute of suffering love. "The world is better," says Richard Swinburne in a fine passage,

if agents pay proper tribute to losses and failures, if they are sad at the failure of their endeavours, mourn for the death of a child, are angry at the seduction of a wife, and so on. Such emotions involve suffering and anguish, but in having such proper feelings a man shows his respect to himself and others. A man who feels no grief at the death of his child or the seduction of his wife is rightly branded by us as insensitive, for he has failed to pay the proper tribute of feeling to others, to show in his feeling how much he values them, and thereby failed to value them properly—for valuing them properly involves having proper reactions of feeling to their loss.[12]

Suffering is an essential element in that mode of life which says not only "No" to the misery of our world but "Yes" to its glories.

And if one does pay to friends and relatives the tribute of a love that may suffer, then also one will struggle to prolong their lives rather than to reorient a self cast into suffering by the snuffing out of their lives. If one does pay to justice among one's people the tribute of a love that may suffer, then also one will struggle to overthrow the tyrant rather than to reconstruct one's self so as to be content under tyranny. Suffering contributes to changing the world. Suffering must sometimes be cultivated. We are indeed to live in a solidarity of grieving and rejoicing—but of grieving and rejoicing over the absence and presence of that mode of human flourishing which the biblical writers call *shalom*; not just over the religious condition of our souls.

This, I said, was a different way to go—the way of "No" to death rather than to love of that which dies, the way of "No" to injustice rather than to love of justice, the way of "No" to poverty rather than to the struggle to alleviate poverty—and Yes, the way of "No" to our distance from God rather than to love of God. It is also, in my judgment, a better way. For it is in line with God's suffering and with God's joy. Instead of loving only God we will love what God loves, including God. For it is in the presence of justice and shalom among his human creatures that God delights, as it is for the full realization of justice and shalom in his perfected Kingdom that he works. To love what is of worth in this world and to suffer over its destruction is to pay to that Kingdom the tribute of anguish over its delay. "Our hearts are restless until they find their rest in thee, O Lord," said Augustine. What must be added is that our hearts will not find their full rest and *should not* find their full rest until the heart of our Lord is itself fully at rest in his perfected Kingdom.

Notes

1. Translated by R. S. Pine-Coffin (Harmondsworth, Middlesex: Penguin Books, 1961). All my citations from the *Confessions* will be from this translation.

2. No doubt for the reason which is vividly stated in this passage from Plotinus:

And so this being, [Love Eros] has from everlasting come into existence from the soul's aspiration towards the higher and the good, and he was there always, as long as Soul, too, existed. And he is a mixed thing, having a part of need, in that he wishes to be filled, but not without a share of plenitude, in that he seeks what is wanting to that which he already has; for certainly that which is altogether without a share in the good would not ever seek the good. So he is born of Plenty and Poverty. . . . But his mother is Poverty, because aspiration belongs to that which is in need. (*Enneads* III, 5, 9; Armstrong tr. in Loeb Classical Library [Cambridge, Mass.: Harvard University Press, 1967])

For arguments that the *full* notion of *eros* in Plato and Plotinus included some component of self-giving, see A. H. Armstrong, "Platonic Eros and Christian Agape" in Armstrong, *Plotinian and Christian Studies* (London: Variorum Reprints, 1979); and John M. Rist, *Eros and Psyche: Studies in Plato, Plotinus and Origen* (Toronto: University of Toronto Press, 1964).

3. In the above I follow A. C. Lloyd, "Emotion and Decision in Stoic Psychology" in John M. Rist (ed.) *The Stoics* (Berkeley, Calif.: University of California Press, 1978). Compare the summary by A. A. Long, *Hellenistic Philosophy* (New York: Charles Scribner's Sons, 1974), pp. 206–207:

The Stoic sage is free from all passion. Anger, anxiety, cupidity, dread, elation, these and similar extreme emotions are all absent from his disposition. He does not regard pleasure as something good, nor pain as something evil. . . . The Stoic sage is not insensitive to painful or pleasurable sensations, but they do not 'move his soul excessively'. He is impassive towards them. But he is not entirely impassive. . . . His disposition is characterized by 'good emotional states'. Well-wishing, wishing another man good things for his sake; joy: rejoicing in virtuous actions, a tranquil life, a good conscience. . . ; and 'wariness', reasonable disinclination.

Augustine himself, in various scattered passages, uses the classic Stoic concept of *pathos*. He speaks, for example, of "that state which the Greeks call pathos, whence our word passion is derived; *pathos*, and passion, being a motion of the mind against reason" (*City of God*

VIII, 16). Using this definition, one would have to express Augustine's interpretation of the Stoic position as that such a perturbing 'phenomenon' as fear or grief might or might not, in a given case, be a pathos. It would be so if it overthrew the rule of reason in the person experiencing it; otherwise it would not be. And then to say that the wise person is characterized by apathy would be to say that such perturbing 'phenomena' as fear and grief would not function in him as passions; it would not be to say that he never experiences these.

4. Quoted in J. K. Mozley, *The Impassible God* (Cambridge: Cambridge University Press, 1926), pp. 165–166. Compare these passages from Hartshorne: "The lover is not merely the one who unwaveringly understands and tries to help; the lover is just as emphatically the one who takes unto himself the varying joys and sorrows of others, and whose own happiness is capable of alteration thereby. . . . Love *is* joy in the joy (actual or expected) of another, and sorrow in the sorrow of another" (*Man's Vision of God* [New York: Harper & Bros., 1941], pp. 111, 116). "Sympathetic dependence is a sign of excellence and waxes with every ascent in the scale of being. Joy calls for sympathetic joy, sorrow for sympathetic sorrow, as the most excellent possible forms of response to these states. The eminent form of sympathetic dependence can only apply to deity, for this form cannot be less than an omniscient sympathy, which depends upon and is exactly colored by every nuance of joy or sorrow anywhere in the world" (*The Divine Relativity: A Social Conception of God* [New Haven, Yale University Press, 1964], p. 48).

5. See, for example, Anselm in *Proslogion* 8: "How art Thou at once pitiful and impassible? For if Thou art impassible, Thou dost not suffer with man; if Thou dost not suffer with man, Thy heart is not wretched by compassion with the wretched, which is the meaning of being pitiful. But if Thou are not pitiful, whence can the wretched gain so great comfort? How then art Thou, and art Thou not pitiful, Lord, except that Thou are pitiful in respect of us, and not in respect of Thyself? Truly Thou art so in respect of our feeling, and art not in respect of Thine. For when Thou lookest upon us in our wretchedness we feel the effect of Thy pity, Thou feelest not the effect. And therefore Thou art pitiful, because Thou savest the wretched, and sparest the sinners who belong to Thee; and Thou are

not pitiful, because Thou art touched by no fellow-suffering in that wretchedness." And Aquinas in *Summa theologiae* I, 19, a. 11, resp.: "When certain human passions are predicted of the Godhead metaphorically, this is done because of a likeness in the effect. Hence a thing that is in us a sign of some passion is signified metaphorically in God under the name of that passion. Thus with us it is usual for an angry man to punish, so that punishment becomes an expression of anger. Therefore punishment itself is signified with anger, when anger is attributed to God."

   6. Quoted in Mozley, p. 105.

   7. Ibid., p. 106.

   8. Ibid., p. 106–107.

   9. William Lyons, *Emotion* (Cambridge: Cambridge University Press, 1980).

   10. So when Aquinas speaks of God's *mercy* (*misericordia*), he has no choice but to turn it into mere benevolence: "Mercy is especially to be attributed to God, provided it be considered in its effect, but not as an affection to passion. In proof of which it must be observed that a person is said to be merciful [*misericors*] as being, so to speak, sorrowful at heart [*miserum cor*]; in other words, as being affected with sorrow at the misery of another as though it were his own. Hence it follows that he endeavors to dispel the misery of this other, as if it were his; and this is the effect of mercy. To sorrow therefore, over the misery of others does not belong to God; but it does most properly belong to Him to dispel that misery, whatever be the effect we call misery" (*ST* I, 21, a. 3, resp.).

   11. For a full consideration of our topic, there is an argument of Charles Hartshorne which would have to be considered. He argues that God's *benevolence* must itself be understood as a suffering love—or strictly speaking, as a love that yields suffering. For God in His benevolence wants his human creatures to be happy. Yet so often they are not. God suffers, then from the frustration of his benevolent intention. This, of course, is something that the tradition would never have granted: God's benevolent intention could be frustrated. Theologians, says Hartshorne,

   sought to maintain a distinction between love as a desire, with an element of possible gain or loss to the self, and love as purely altruistic benevolence; or again between sensuous and spiritual love, *eros* and *agape*. . . . Benevolence *is* desire for the welfare of others. . . . Of course it must be a superrationally enlightened, an all-comprehending, never wearying desire for others' good, that is attributed to God. But still desire, so far as that means partial dependence for extent of happiness upon the happiness of others. . . . Lincoln's desire that the slaves might be free was not less desire because it was spiritual, or less spiritual because it was desire—that is a wish, *capable of being painfully disappointed or happily fulfilled*

To hold that God "wills" or purposes human welfare, but is absolutely untouched by the realization or non-realization of this or that portion of the purposed goal (due, for instance, to human sins or unfortunate use of free will), seems just nonsense. . . .

Does this not introduce the tragedy of unfulfilled desire into God? Yes, it does just that.

(Charles Hartshorne, *Man's Vision of God* [New York: Harper & Brothers, 1941], pp. 116, 135, 294). Compare Fretheim, in *Suffering of God*, p. 134: "In terms of Jeremiah 45, we need to speak in some sense of a temporary failure in what God has attempted to do in the world. Because of this, the mourners should take up a lamentation for God as well."

12. Richard Swinburne, *The Existence of God* (Oxford: Oxford University Press, 1979), p. 192.

TEN

𝓔𝓔𝓔

DOES GOD CHANGE?

William Hasker

The claim that God is timelessly eternal, until recently a majority view among orthodox Christian theists, has suffered massive defections in recent years. Still, the doctrine of divine timelessness continues to enjoy . . . acceptance among philosophers . . . and it may retain even more of its popularity among theologians. So it may be worthwhile to state briefly the reasons for preferring the view that God is temporal—that he lives and interacts with us through the changes of time.[1] First of all, it is clear that the doctrine of divine timelessness is not taught in the Bible and does not reflect the way the biblical writers understood God. In spite of appeals by defenders of the doctrine to texts such as Exodus 3:14, John 8:58 and 2 Peter 3:8, there simply is no trace in the Scripture of the elaborate metaphysical and conceptual apparatus that is required to make sense of divine timelessness.[2] On the positive side, the biblical writers undeniably do present God as living, acting and reacting in time, as Nicholas Wolterstorff has powerfully argued.[3]

In the face of this, the defender of timelessness has to say either that the scriptural texts do not mean what they seem plainly to say or that what they say (and mean) is, strictly speaking, false: what they say may be adequate for the religious needs of simple people, but the truly enlightened must think of God rather in the categories of timeless eternity while still (no doubt) "speaking with the masses" in ordinary religious contexts so as not to give offense to those who are not up to the rigors of proper theology. Now it might possibly be acceptable to say this sort of thing if there were clear and compelling reasons for preferring divine timelessness to taking the Scriptures at face value. But if such reasons are lacking, it seems much better to take the Bible at its word and to understand God as a temporal being.

The other main difficulty about divine timelessness is that it is very hard to make clear logical sense of the doctrine. If God is truly timeless, so that temporal determinations of "before" and "after" do not apply to him, then how can God *act* in time, as the Scriptures say that he does? How can he *know* that is occurring on the changing earthly scene? How can he *respond* when his children turn to him in prayer and obedience? And above all, if God is timeless and incapable of change, how can God be born, grow up, live with and among people, suffer and die, as we believe he did as incarnated in Jesus? Whether there are good answers to these questions, whether the doctrine of divine timelessness is intelligible and logically coherent, and whether it can be reconciled with central Christian beliefs such as the incarnation remain matters of intense controversy.[4]

But even if divine timelessness is not incoherent and not in conflict with other key beliefs, it seems that we have at best only a tenuous grasp on the conception of God as a timeless being.[5] Once again, this might be something we could have to accept, *if* there were compelling reasons forcing us to affirm divine timelessness. But do such reasons exist? I think not. . . .

In the philosophical lineage stretching from Parmenides to Plato to Plotinus, there is a strong metaphysical and valuational preference for permanence over change. True Being, in this tradition, must of necessity be changeless; whatever changes, on the other hand, enjoys a substandard sort of being if any at all—at best it may be, in Plato's lovely phrase, a "moving image of eternity." And this bias against change has been powerfully influential in classical theology, leading to the insistence on an excessively strong doctrine of divine immutability—which, in turn, provides key support for divine timelessness, since timelessness is the most effective way (and perhaps the only way) to rule out, once and for all, the possibility of any change in God.

For us moderns, this preference for permanence over change is scarcely compelling. Indeed, it is arguable that in our intellectual life as well as in our general culture the pendulum has swung too far in the other direction, so that if anything at all remains constant for a while our response is one of boredom and impatience. Be that as it may, the extreme valuational preference for immutability has little hold on our thinking, and the appeal of theological doctrines based on this valuation is weakened accordingly.

Finally, let us consider the doctrine of divine impassibility—the claim that God's perfection requires that God be completely self-contained, not influenced or conditioned in any way by creatures, and in particular incapable of any suffering, distress or negative emotions of any kind.[6] One of the more extreme versions of impassibility appears in Aristotle's claim that God, being perfect, cannot take any notice of lesser beings such as humans; a perfect Thinker must be one that thinks only perfect thoughts, which means that God is eternally engaged in reflecting on his own thoughts: "His thinking is a thinking of thinking." This view is so clearly in conflict with a Christian understanding of God that it has never, to my knowledge, been adopted by Christian thinkers. But in slightly less extreme forms, divine impassibility has left a lasting imprint on Christian theology. Thus, Anselm addresses God as follows: "Thou art both compassionate, because thou dost save the wretched, and spare those who sin against thee; and not compassionate, because thou art affected by no sympathy for wretchedness" (*Proslogium* 7). Plainly stated, this says that God *acts* as we would expect a compassionate person to act—but the *feeling* of compassion forms no part of the divine life and experience.

On this point, also, Nicholas Wolterstorff makes an important contribution when he connects Augustine's doctrine of divine impassibility with Augustine's own reaction at the death of a friend.[7] Augustine was endowed with a nature that was richly emotional as well as intellectually powerful, and he speaks in moving terms of the void left in his life by the departure of his friend. Yet he also severely criticizes this love of his, "a love so intense for a being so fragile that its destruction could cause such grief."[8] Such an excess of "worldly affection," he thought, should have no part in the life of the Christian—and later on, at the death of his mother, Augustine attempted (though without complete success) to restrain himself from any overt expression of grief.

Few of us today share Augustine's view of these matters. Common experience shows us (and is reinforced by psychology) that the suppression of grief is a poor strategy—that the "work of grieving" needs to be done lest one carry the grief unresolved for years to come. And the suggestion that we should not care deeply for our fellow human beings because if we care too much we expose ourselves to suffering causes us to shake our heads sadly and turn away.

But it is hard to avoid the logic of the connection Augustine makes between the ideal of human life and the perfection of God's life. If the majestic and supremely admirable Lord of all is "without passion"—if he views the world and all its sorrows and sufferings with serene, imperturbable bliss—then should not this be our aim as well? Conversely, if it is fitting and good that we humans should care deeply for one another, should love one another in a way that makes us vulnerable to suffering and loss, then should not a love like this be attributed to God also? Perhaps the two ideals, of human and divine love, could be pried apart—but only at the cost of voiding the scriptural injunction to be "imitators of God" (Eph 5:1).

In order to give greater focus to the considerations of this section, it may be helpful to examine in some detail an argument for divine immutability that has been prevalent since the time of Plato. If God were to change, so the argument goes, then he would change either for the better or for the worse. But God cannot change for the better, since he is already perfect. And he cannot change for the worse, for this would mean that he would no longer be perfect. So God cannot change.

A first point to notice is that this argument is an instance of "perfect being" theology. That is, the assumption is made that God is an absolutely perfect being—in Anselm's phrase, "the being than which nothing greater can be conceived"—and then conclusions concerning God's attributes are drawn from this assumption. Clearly, perfect being theology is operative, both explicitly and implicitly, at many, many points in the theological tradition.[9]

I believe the assumption that God is an absolutely perfect being is proper and correct. It does seem to be part of our conception of God that God is deserving of absolute, unreserved and unconditional worship and devotion. But suppose that we were to discover that God was in some significant way deficient and imperfect—suppose, for example, that God's attitude toward humans was a harshly demanding one that took little or no account of our needs and frailties. We might still worship God in spite of this "fault" on God's part—but would our worship not be tinged with disappointment, with regret for what "might have been" had God not suffered from this particular imperfection? But a worship tinged with such regret is not an expression of "absolute, unreserved and unconditional devotion." I think we do well to reject such possibilities and to see in God the sum of all perfections.

The difficulties with perfect being theology do not, in my view, stem from the assumption that God is an absolutely perfect being—that he is "whatever it is better to be than not to be." Rather, difficulties have arisen because people have been too ready to assume that they can determine, easily and with little effort, what perfection *is* in the case of God—that is, what attributes a perfect being must possess. Yet it clearly is no simple matter to say what is the best kind of life for a human being or what are the ideal attributes (or virtues) for a human being to possess. So why should we assume that this is simple in the case of God? I do not think it should be taken as obvious, without long and thoughtful consideration, that it is "better" for God to be temporal *or* timeless, mutable *or* immutable, passible *or* impassible. So if we are going to object to Plato's argument, we need not reject perfect being theology as such; rather, it is the application the argument makes of divine perfection that we must question.

And we can indeed question the application in this case. In fact, Plato's argument is straightforwardly fallacious, because it rests on a false dichotomy. It rests on the assumption that all change is either for the better or for the worse, an assumption that is simply false. Consider the operation of an extremely accurate watch. A short while ago, it registered the time as five minutes after six o'clock, but now it registers twelve minutes after six. Clearly, this is a change in the watch. (Compare this watch with an "immutable" watch that always registers 10:37, day in and day out.) Is this a change for the better, suggesting a previous state of imperfection? Not at all; the watch when it registered 6:05 was perfectly accurate. Is it then a change for the worse, a decline from perfection? Again, this is clearly not the case: the time now *is* 6:12, and the watch would be inaccurate, run down or broken if it failed to register that time. So there are changes that are neither for the better nor for the worse, and the change in the watch is such a change. It is, in fact, an example of *a change that is consistent with and/or required by a constant state of excellence.*

This is not to say that the changes that occur in God are all like the changes in the watch. There are such changes in God, to be sure: God always knows what time it is. But there are other, more significant changes in God that go far beyond simply "tracking" a changing situation. When I do something wrong, God comes to be in a state of knowing that I am doing something wrong, and this is a change in God. (He could not have known ten minutes ago that I was doing something wrong, because I was not doing wrong ten minutes ago.) God also becomes displeased with me, in a way he was not before, and he may initiate actions toward me designed to remedy the situation. (For instance, the Holy Spirit may begin working in my life in such a way as to bring me to repentance for the wrong I have done.) Turning to a broader context, when God began to create the universe he changed, beginning to do something that previously he had not done. This act of creation, our faith tells us, is not something that was required in order for God to be perfect in every respect; it was sheerly a matter of free choice for God whether to create at all. Such a change, then, is consistent with, though not required by, God's maintaining a constant state of perfection.

But it is time to bring this section to a close. We have reviewed a series of divine attributes with regard to which the theology of divine openness reaches different conclusions from the classical theory of a God who is totally self-contained and unconditioned by his creation. God, we want to say, exists and carries on his life in time; he undergoes changing states. And this means that God changes—not indeed in his essential nature, his love and wisdom and power and faithfulness, but in his thoughts and deeds toward us and the rest of his creation, matching his thoughts toward the creature with the creature's actual state at the time God thinks of it. And finally, God is not impassive and unmoved by his creation; rather, in deciding to create us and love us God has opened himself to the possibility of joy and sorrow, depending on what happens to us and especially on how we respond to his love and grace.

Notes

1. The core of what I mean by saying that God is "in time" is that God experiences changing mental states. Physical time—time as measured by physical changes, such as the rotation of planets or the vibrations of quartz crystals—did not exist prior to or apart from the creation of those physical realities by which it is measured. And conventional time—calendar time and clock time—depends for its existence on the human beings who adopted the conventions. But apart from all of this we can maintain that a change of state and therefore of time, does exist in God, who is thus present in every "now" of time rather than in the "eternal Now."

2. The case that the scriptural conception is not of a timeless God is made forcefully by Alan G. Padgett in *God, Eternity and the Nature of Time* (New York: St. Martins's Press, 1992), chap. 2.

3. See Nicholas Wolterstorff, "God Everlasting," in *God and the Good*, ed. Clifton J. Orlebeke and Lewis B. Smedes (Grand Rapids, Mich.: Eerdmans, 1975). [See this volume, pp. 111–36.]

4. In chap. 8 of *God, Time and Knowledge* (Ithaca, N.Y.: Cornell University Press, 1989; referred to hereafter as *GTK*), I argue that the doctrine of divine timelessness has not been shown to be logically incoherent; in chap. 9 I give my own reasons for rejecting the doctrine. Alan Padgett gives a strong critique of divine timelessness in *God, Eternity and the Nature of Time*.

5. My own observation is that many who affirm divine timelessness have hardly begun to think through such questions, and in fact what they say on the topic often leaves one more or less in the dark concerning what they understand the doctrine of divine timelessness to mean. As an example, consider the *Systematic Theology*, 3rd ed., by the well-respected Reformed theologian Louis Berkhof (Grand Rapids, Mich.: Eerdmans, 1946). Berkhof defines eternity as *"that perfection of God whereby He is elevated above all temporal limits and all suc-*

cession of moments, and possesses the whole of His existence in one indi-visible present" (p. 60, emphasis his). But throughout the volume Berkhof consistently speaks about God and his actions in temporal language; concerning such questions as those raised in the text, he says only that "the relation of eternity to time constitutes one of the most difficult problems in philosophy and theology, perhaps incapable of solution in our present condition" (ibid.). It seems to me that the doctrine of timelessness is not a living part of Berkhof's theology but rather a mere remnant of tradition—a tradition that he might better have reexamined critically.

6. The best recent book on this topic is Richard Creel, *Divine Impassibility* (Cambridge: Cambridge University Press, 1986). Creel defends a modified version of impassibility, but in other respects his conclusions about God are very much in harmony with those presented in these pages.

7. Nicholas Wolterstorff, "Suffering Love," in *Philosophy and the Christian Faith*, ed. Thomas V. Morris (Notre Dame, Ind.: University of Notre Dame Press, 1988), pp. 196–237. [See this volume, pp. 111–36—Eds.]

8. Ibid., p. 196 (the words quoted are Wolterstorff's). [See this volume, p. 112.]

9. A good recent discussion of perfect being theology may be found in Thomas V. Morris, *Anselmian Explorations* (Notre Dame, Ind.: University of Notre Dame Press, 1987).

ELEVEN

DOES GOD KNOW THE FUTURE?

Steven M. Cahn

In the Book of Deuteronomy, God says to the people of Israel, "I have put before you life and death, blessing and curse. Choose life—if you and your offspring would live. . . ."[1] Did God know which option the people would choose? If so, how could their choice have been free? For if God knew they would choose life, then to have chosen death would have confuted God's knowledge—which is impossible. If God knew they would choose death, then to have chosen life would also have confuted God's knowledge. But God gave the people a genuine choice. So even God did not know how they would choose.

I find this line of argument persuasive, but many notable thinkers have believed it unsound. In what follows I shall present briefly a sampling of their objections and my replies.

Objection 1. "Just as your memory does not force the past to have happened, God's foreknowledge does not force the future to happen." So argued St. Augustine.[2]

Reply. Admittedly, my remembering that an event occurred does not cause the event's occurrence. And God's foreknowledge that an event will occur does not cause its occurrence. But if I know that an event occurred, then it is not within my power to alter its occurrence. Not only won't I alter it, I can't.

Similarly, if God knows that an event will occur, then it is not within God's power to alter its occurrence. Even assuming God is all-powerful, God can only do what is logically possible, for what is logically impossible is incoherent, and an incoherent task is no task at all. Thus, if an event will occur, even if God does not cause its occurrence, God is bound by logic to allow its occurrence. In short, knowledge does not cause events, but, given definitive knowledge of events, they are unavoidable.

Objection 2. "[W]e estimate the intimacy of relationship between two persons by the foreknowledge one has of the action of the other, without supposing that in either case the one or the other's freedom has thereby been endangered. So even divine foreknowledge cannot endanger freedom." So said the German theologian Friedrich Schleiermacher.[3]

Reply. We rarely claim more than strong belief about what others will do, for we realize that however likely our prediction, we may be proved wrong. But when we do possess knowledge, it is incompatible with free choice. For example, we know we all shall die. It follows that it is not within anyone's power to remain alive forever. If we knew not only *that* we would die but also when, where, and how we would die, then we could not avoid death in the known time, place, and manner. Strong beliefs can be confuted, but not knowledge.

Objection 3. "It is not true, then, that because God foreknew what would be within the power of our wills, nothing therefore lies within the power of our wills. For when He foreknew this, He did not foreknow nothing. Therefore, if He who foreknew what would lie within the power of our wills did not foreknow nothing, but something, then clearly something lies within in the power of our wills even though God has foreknowledge of it." Again, St. Augustine.[4]

Reply. This line of reasoning begs the question, assuming what is supposed to be proved. If God foreknew our free choices, then they would be free. But can God foreknow our free choices? The argument I presented originally concludes that God cannot foreknow our free choices. Simply assuming the possibility of such foreknowledge carries no weight against the argument and identifies no mistake in it.

Objection 4. "[S]ince God lives in the eternal present, His knowledge transcends all movement of time and abides in the simplicity of its immediate present. It encompasses the infinite sweep of past and future, and regards all things in its simple comprehension as if they were now taking place. Thus, if you will think about the foreknowledge by which God distinguishes all things, you will rightly consider it to be not a foreknowledge of future events, but knowledge of a never changing present." So argued the Roman philosopher Boethius.[5]

Reply. We make certain choices before others. Indeed, certain choices presuppose others. For example, the choice to seek a divorce requires a prior choice to marry. Whatever is meant by the assertion that God transcends time (a murky claim), God presumably knows that we make certain choices before others. So God takes account of time. Admittedly, God is supposed to view the future as clearly as we view the present. But appeals to the clarity of God's knowledge only underscore why that knowledge is incompatible with the freedom of choices we are yet to make.

Objection 5. "[T]hough we do not know the true nature of God's knowledge . . . yet we know that . . . nothing of all existing things is hidden from Him and that His knowledge of them does not change their nature, but the possible retains its nature as a possibility. Anything in this enumeration that appears contradictory is so only owing to the structure of our knowledge, which has nothing in common with His knowledge except the name." So wrote the medieval Jewish sage Maimonides.[6]

Reply. If God's knowledge has nothing in common with human knowledge, then God's knowledge, unlike human knowledge, would not imply the truth of what is known. So God's knowledge, whatever its nature, may be compatible with free choice but only in some sense not relevant to the original argument. If we do not understand the meaning of the words we use, we cannot use them to make claims we understand.

Suppose now that the argument with which I began can be sustained in the face of all criticisms (and much more can be said on both sides). Does it follow that God lacks omniscience? Not if one adopts the view, which some commentators have attributed to Aristotle,[7] that statements about future choices are neither true nor false, but, at present, indeterminate. According to this view, it is not now true you will finish reading this entire book and not true you won't. Until you decide, the matter is indeterminate.

As the medieval Jewish philosopher Gersonides argued, to be omniscient is to know every true statement. Since it is not true you will finish reading the entire book and not true you won't, but true that the matter is indeterminate, an omniscient being does not know you will finish reading and does not know you won't, but does know the whole truth, namely, that the matter is indeterminate and depends on your free choice.

Thus, assuming God is omniscient, God knows the entire physical structure of the universe but not the outcome of free choices. As Gersonides wrote, "[T]he fact that God does not have the knowledge of which possible outcome will be realized does not imply any defect in God (may He be blessed). For perfect knowledge of something is the knowledge of what that thing is in reality; when the thing is not apprehended as it is, this is error, not knowledge. Hence, God knows these things in the best manner possible . . ."[8]

In other words, when God offered the people of Israel both life and death, God, although omniscient, did not know which choice they would make. God knew all that was knowable, the whole truth. But the whole truth was that the choice of life or death rested with the people of Israel. They were responsible for their decision. God awaited, but could not foresee, the outcome of their exercise of freedom.

Some may find this view unsettling, since it implies that God's knowledge, while in a sense complete, does not include within its purview definitive answers to all questions about the future. But, like Gersonides, I find this conclusion consistent with the Holy Scriptures. As Gersonides wrote,

> God (may He be blessed), by means of the Prophets, commands men who are about to suffer evil fortune that they mend their ways so that they will avert this punishment. . . . Now this indicates that what God knows of future events is known by Him as not necessarily occurring.[9]

In short, divine warnings imply uncertain outcomes.

I conclude with an admission. Certain Biblical passages may suggest, contrary to what I have argued, that God knows the future in all its details, including the outcome of future free choices. If such textual evidence were presented, how would I respond? I would echo Gersonides: "If the literal sense of the Torah differs from reason, it is necessary to interpret these passages in accordance with the demands of reason."[10] The task of developing such interpretations, if required, I leave to others.

Notes

1. *Tanakh: The Holy Scriptures* (Philadelphia: Jewish Publication Society, 1988), Deuteronomy 30:19.

2. Thomas Williams, trans., *On Free Choice of the Will* (Indianapolis: Hackett, 1993), Book III, sec. 4, p. 78.

3. H. R. Mackintosh and J. S. Stewart, eds., *The Christian Faith* (Edinburgh: T. And T. Clark 1928), p. 228.

4. R. W. Dyson, trans., *The City of God Against the Pagans* (Cambridge: Cambridge University Press, 1998), Book V, sec. 10, p. 205.

5. Richard Green, trans., *The Consolation of Philosophy* (New York: Library of Liberal Arts, 1962), Book 5, prose 6, p. 116.

6. Chaim Rabin, trans., *The Guide of the Perplexed* (Indianapolis: Hackett, 1995), p. 163.

7. See, for example, Richard Taylor, "The Problem of Future Contingencies," *Philosophical Review* 66 (1957), pp. 1–28.

8. Seymour Feldman, trans., *The Wars of the Lord* (Philadelphia: Jewish Publication Society, 1987), vol. 2, p. 118.

9. Ibid. p. 118.

10. Ibid. p. 98.

TWELVE

DO ALL RELIGIONS WORSHIP
THE SAME GOD?

John Hick

Let me begin by proposing a working definition of religion as an understanding of the universe, together with an appropriate way of living within it, which involves reference beyond the natural world to God or gods or to the Absolute or to a transcendent order or process. Such a definition includes such theistic faiths as Judaism, Christianity, Islam, Sikhism; the theistic Hinduism of the Bhagavad Gītī; the semi-theistic faith of Mahayana Buddhism and the non-theistic faiths of Theravada Buddhism and non-theistic Hinduism. It does not however include purely naturalistic systems of belief, such as communism and humanism, immensely important though these are today as alternatives to religious life.

When we look back into he past we find that religion has been a virtually universal dimension of human life—so much so that man has been defined as the religious animal. For he has displayed an innate tendency to experience his environment as being religiously as well as naturally significant, and to feel required to live in it as such. To quote anthropologist Raymond Firth, "religion is universal in human societies."[1] "In every human community on earth today," says Wilfred Cantwell Smith, "there exists something that we, as sophisticated observers, may term religion, or a religion. And we are able to see it in each case as the latest development in a continuous tradition that goes back, we can now affirm, for at least one hundred thousand years."[2] In the life of primitive man this religious tendency is expressed in a belief in sacred objects endowed with *mana*, and in a multitude of nature and ancestral spirits needing to be carefully propitiated. The divine was here crudely apprehended as a plurality of quasi-animal forces which could to some extent be controlled by ritualistic and magical procedures. This represents the simplest beginning of man's awareness of the transcendent in the infancy of the human race—an infancy which is also to some extent still available for study in the life of primitive tribes today.

The development of religion and religions begins to emerge into the light of recorded history as the third millennium B.C. moves toward the period around 2000 B.C. There are two main regions of the earth in which civilisation seems first to have arisen and in which religions first took a shape that is at least dimly discernible to us as we peer back through the mists of time—these being Mesopotamia in the Near East and the Indus valley of northern India. In Mesopotamia men lived in nomadic shepherd tribes, each worshipping its own god. Then the tribes gradually coalesced into nation states, the former tribal gods becoming ranked in hierarchies (some however being lost by amalgamation in the process) dominated by great national deities such as Marduk of Babylon, the Sumerian Ishtar, Amon of Thebes, Jahweh of Israel, the Greek Zeus, and so on. Further east in the Indus valley there was likewise a wealth of gods and goddesses, though apparently not so much tribal or national in character as expressive of the basic forces of nature, above all fertility. The many deities of the Near East and of India expressed man's awareness of the divine at the dawn of documentary history, some four thousand years ago. It is perhaps worth stressing that the picture was by no means a wholly pleasant one. The tribal and national gods were often martial and cruel, sometimes requiring human sacrifices. And although rather little is known about the very early, pre-Aryan Indian deities, it is certain that later Indian deities have vividly symbolised the cruel and destructive as well as the beneficent aspects of nature.

These early developments in the two cradles of civilisation, Mesopotamia and the Indus valley, can be described as the growth of natural religion, prior to any special intrusions of divine revelation or illumination. Primitive spirit-worship expressed man's fears of unknown forces; his reverence for nature deities expressed his sense of dependence upon realities greater than himself; and his tribal gods expressed the unity and continuity of his group over against other groups. One can in fact discern all sorts of casual connections between the forms which early religion took and the material circumstances of man's life, indicating the large part played by the human element within the history of religion. For example, Trevor Ling points out that life in ancient India (apart from the Punjab immediately prior to the Aryan invasions) was agricultural and was organised in small village units; and suggests that "among agricultural peoples, aware of the fertile earth which brings forth from itself and nourishes its progeny upon its broad bosom, it is the mother-principle which seems important."[3] Accordingly God the Mother, and a variety of more specialised female deities, have always held a prominent place in Indian religious thought and mythology. This contrasts with the characteristically male expression of deity in the Semitic religions, which had their origins among nomadic, pastoral, herd-keeping peoples in the Near East. The divine was known to the desert-dwelling herdsmen who founded the Israelite tradition as God the King and Father; and this conception has continued both in later Judaism and in Christianity, and was renewed out of the desert experience of Mohammed in the Islamic religion. Such regional variations in our human ways of conceiving the divine have persisted through time into the developed world faiths that we know today. The typical western conception of God is still predominantly in terms of the male principle of power and authority; and in the typical Indian conceptions of deity the female principle still plays a distinctly larger part than in the west.

Here then was the natural condition of man's religious life: religion without revelation. But sometime around 800 B.C. there began what has been called the golden age of religious creativity. This consisted in a remarkable series of revelatory experiences occurring during the next five hundred or so years in different parts of the world, experiences which deepened and purified men's conception of the ultimate, and which religious faith can only attribute to the pressure of the divine Spirit upon the human spirit. First came the early Jewish prophets, Amos, Hosea and first Isaiah, declaring that they had heard the Word of the Lord claiming their obedience and demanding a new level of righteousness and justice in the life of Israel. Then in Persia the great prophet Zoroaster appeared; China produced Lao-tzu and then Confucius; in India the Upanishads were written, and Gotama the Buddha lived, and Mahavira, the founder of the Jain religion and, probably about the end of this period, the writing of the Bhagavid Gītī,[4] and Greece produced Pythagoras and then, ending this golden age, Socrates and Plato. Then after the gap of some three hundred years came Jesus of Nazareth and the emergence of Christianity; and after another gap the prophet Mohammed and the rise of Islam.

The suggestion that we must consider is that these were all moments of divine revelation. But let us ask, in order to test this thought, whether we should not expect God to make his revelation in a single mighty act, rather than to produce a number of different, and therefore presumably partial, revelations at different times and places? I think that in seeing the answer to this question we receive an important clue to the place of the religions of the world in the divine purpose. For when we remember the facts of history and geography we realise that in the period we are speaking of, between two and three thousand years ago, it was not possible for God to reveal himself through any human mediation to all mankind. A world-wide revelation might be possible today, thanks to the inventions of printing, and even more of radio, TV and communication satellites. But in the technology of the ancient world this was not possible. Although on a time scale of centuries and millennia there has been a slow diffusion and interaction of cultures, particularly within the vast Euro-Asian land mass, yet the more striking fact for our present purpose is the fragmented character of the ancient world. Communications between the different groups of humanity was then so limited and slow that for all practical purposes men inhabited different worlds. For the most part people in Europe, in India, in Arabia, in Africa, in China were unaware of the others' existence. And as the world was fragmented so was its religious life. If there was to be a revelation of the divine reality to mankind it had to be a pluriform revelation, a series of revealing experiences occurring independently within the different streams of human history. And since religion and culture were one, the great creative moments of revelation and illumination have influenced the development of the various cultures, giving them the coherence and impetus to expand into larger units, thus creating the vast, many-sided historical entities which we call the world religions.

Each of these religio-cultural complexes has expanded until it touched the boundaries of another such complex spreading out from another centre. Thus each major occasion of divine revelation has slowly transformed the primitive and national religions within the sphere of its influence into what we now know as the world faiths. The early Dravidian and Aryan polytheisms of India were drawn through the religious experience and thought of the Brahmins into what the west calls Hinduism. The national and mystery cults of the Mediterranean world and then of northern Europe were drawn by influences stemming from the life and teaching of Christ into what has become Christianity. The early polytheism of the Arab peoples has been transformed under the influence of Mohammed and his message into Islam. Great areas of Southeast Asia, of China, Tibet and Japan were drawn into the spreading Buddhist movement. None of these expansions from different centres of revelation has of course been simple and uncontested, and a number of alternatives which proved less durable have perished or been absorbed in the process—for example, Mithraism has disappeared altogether; and Zoroastrianism, whilst it greatly influenced the development of the Judaic-Christian tradition, and has to that extent been absorbed, only survives directly today on a small scale in Parseeism.

Seen in this historical context these movements of faith—the Judaic-Christian, the Buddhist, the Hindu, the Muslim—are not essentially rivals. They began at different times and in different places, and each expanded outwards into the surrounding world of primitive natural religion until most of the world was drawn up into one or other of the great revealed faiths. And once this global pattern had become established it has ever since remained fairly stable. It is true that the process of establishment involved conflict in the case of Islam's entry into India and the virtual expulsion of Buddhism from India in the medieval period, and in the case of Islam's advance into Europe and then its retreat at the end of the medieval period. But since the frontiers of the different world faiths became more or less fixed there has been little penetration of one faith into societies moulded by another. The most successful missionary efforts of the great faiths continue to this day to be "downwards" into the remaining world of relatively primitive religions rather than "sideways" into territories dominated by another world faith. For example, as between Christianity and Islam there has been little more than rather rare individual conversions; but both faiths have successful missions in Africa.

Again, the Christian population of the Indian subcontinent, after more than two centuries of missionary effort, is only about 2.7 percent; but on the other hand the Christian mission in the South Pacific are fairly successful. Thus the general picture, so far as the great world religions is concerned, is that each has gone through an early period of geographical expansion, converting a region of the world from its more primitive religious state, and has thereafter continued in a comparatively settled condition within more or less stable boundaries.

Now it is of course possible to see this entire development from the primitive forms of religion up to and including the great world faiths as the history of man's most persistent illusion, growing from crude fantasies into sophisticated metaphysical speculations. But from the standpoint of religious faith the only reasonable hypothesis is that this historical picture represents a movement of divine self-revelation to mankind. This hypothesis offers a general answer to the question of the relation between the different world religions and of the truths which they embody. It suggests to us that the same divine reality has always been self-revealingly active towards mankind, and that the differences of human response are related to different human circumstances. These circumstances—ethnic, geographical, climatic, economic, sociological, historical—have produced the existing differentiations of human culture, and within each main cultural region the response to the divine has taken its own characteristic forms. In each case the post-primitive response has been initiated by some spiritually outstanding individual or succession of individuals, developing in the course of time into one of the great religio-cultural phenomena which we call the world religions. Thus Islam embodies the main response of the Arabic peoples to the divine reality; Hinduism, the main (though not the only) response of the peoples of India; Buddhism, the main response of the peoples of South-east Asia and parts of northern Asia; Christianity, the main response of the European peoples, both within Europe itself and in their emigrations to the Americas and Australasia.

Thus it is, I think, intelligible historically why the revelation of the divine reality to man, and the disclosure of the divine will for human life, had to occur separately within the different streams of human life. We can see how these revelations took different forms related to the different mentalities of the peoples to whom they came and developed within these different cultures into the vast and many-sided historical phenomena of the world religions.

But let us now ask whether this is intelligible theologically. What about the conflicting truth-claims of the different faiths? Is the divine nature personal or non-personal; does deity become incarnate in the world; are human beings born again and again on earth; is the Bible, or the Koran, or the Bhagavad Gītī the Word of God? If what Christianity says in answer to these questions is true, must not what Hinduism says be to a large extent false? If what Buddhism says is true, must not what Islam says be largely false?

Let us begin with the recognition, which is made in all the main religious traditions, that the ultimate divine reality is infinite and as such transcends the grasp of the human mind. God, to use our Christian term, is infinite. He is not a thing, a part of the universe, existing alongside other things; nor is he a being falling under a certain kind. And therefore he cannot draw boundaries around his nature and say that he is this and no more. If we could fully define God, describing his inner being and his outer limits, this would not be God. The God whom our minds can penetrate and whom our thoughts can circumnavigate is merely a finite and partial image of God.

From this it follows that the different encounters with the transcendent within the different religious traditions may all be encounters with the one infinite reality; though with partially different and overlapping aspects of that reality. This is a very familiar thought in Indian religious literature. We read, for example, in the ancient Rig-Vedas, dating back to perhaps as much as a thousand years before Christ:

> They call it Indra, Mitra, Varuna, and Agni
> And also heavenly, beautiful Garutman:
> The real is one, though sages name it variously.[5]

We might translate this thought into the terms of the faiths represented today in Britain:

> They call it Jahweh, Allah, Krishna, Param Atma,
> And also holy, blessed Trinity:
> The real is one, though sages name it differently.

And in the Bhagavad Gītī the Lord Krishna, the personal God of love, says. "However men approach me, even so do I accept them: for, on all sides, whatever path they may choose is mine."[6]

Again, there is the parable of the blind men and the elephant, said to have been told by the Buddha. An elephant was brought to a group of blind men who had never encountered such an animal before. One felt a leg and reported that an elephant is a great living pillar. Another felt the trunk and reported that an elephant is a great snake. Another felt the tusk and reported that an elephant is like a sharp ploughshare. And so on. And then they all quarrelled together, each claiming that his own account was the truth and therefore all the others false. In fact of course they were all true, but each referring only to one aspect of the total reality and all expressed in very imperfect analogies.

Now the possibility, indeed the probability, that we have seriously to consider is that many different accounts of the divine reality may be true, though all expressed in imperfect human analogies, but that none is "the truth, the whole truth, and nothing but the truth." May it not be that the different concepts of God, as Jahweh, Allah, Krishna, Param Atma, Holy Trinity, and so on: and likewise the different concepts of the hidden structure of reality, as the eternal emanation of Brahman or as an immense cosmic process culminating in Nirvana, are all images of the divine, each expressing some aspect or range of aspects and yet none by itself fully and exhaustively corresponding to the infinite nature of the ultimate reality?

Two immediate qualifications however to this hypothesis. First, the idea that we are considering is not that any and every conception of God or of the transcendent is valid, still less all equally valid; but that every conception of the divine which has come out of a great revelatory religious experience and has been tested through a long tradition of worship, and has sustained human faith over centuries of time and in millions of lives, is likely to represent a genuine encounter with the divine reality. And second, the parable of the blind men and the elephant is of course only a parable and like most parables it is designed to make one point and must not be pressed as an analogy at other points. The suggestion is not that the different encounters with the divine which lie at the basis of the great religious traditions are responses to different *parts* of the divine. They are rather encounters from different historical and cultural standpoints with the same infinite divine reality and as such they lead to differently focused awareness of the reality. The indications of this are most evident in worship and prayer. What is said about God in the theological treatises of the different faiths is indeed often widely different. But it is in prayer that a belief in God comes alive and does its main work. And when we turn from abstract theology to the living stuff of worship we meet again and again the overlap and confluence of faiths.

Here, for example, is a Muslim prayer at the feast of Ramadan:

Praise be to God, Lord of creation, Source of all livelihood, who orders the morning, Lord of majesty and honour, of grace and beneficence. He who is so far that he may not be seen and so near that he witnesses the secret things. Blessed be he and for ever exalted.[7]

And here is a Sikh creed used at the morning prayer:

There is but one God. He is all that is.
He is the Creator of all things and He is all-pervasive.
He is without fear and without enmity.
He is timeless, unborn and self-existent.
He is the Enlightener
And can be realised by grace of Himself alone.
He was in the beginning; He was in all ages.
The True One is, was, O Nanak, and shall forever be.[8]

And here again is a verse from the Koran:

To God belongs the praise. Lord of the heavens and Lord of the earth, the Lord of all being. He is the dominion in the heavens and in the earth: he is the Almighty, the All-wise.[9]

Turning now to the Hindu idea of the many incarnations of God, here is a verse from the Rāmāyana:

Seers and sages, saints and hermits, fix on Him their reverent gaze,
And in faint and trembling accents, holy scripture hymns His praise.
He the omnipresent spirit, lord of heaven and earth and hell,
To redeem His people, freely has vouchsafed with men to dwell.[10]

And from the rich literature of devotional song here is a Bhakti hymn of the Vaishnavite branch of Hinduism:

Now all my days with joy I'll fill, full to the brim
With all my heart to Vitthal cling, and only Him.

He will sweep utterly away all dole and care;
And all in sunder shall I rend illusion's snare.
O altogether dear is He, and He alone,
For all my burden He will take to be His own.
Lo, all the sorrow of the world will straightway cease,
And all unending now shall be the reign of peace.[11]

And a Muslim mystical verse:

> Love came a guest
> Within my breast,
> My soul was spread,
> Love banqueted.[12]

And finally another Hindu (Vaishnavite) devotional hymn:

> O save me, save me, Mightiest,
>   Save me and set me free.
> O let the love that fills my breast
>   Cling to thee lovingly.
> Grant me to taste how sweet thou art;
>   Grant me but this, I pray.
> And never shall my love depart
>   Or turn from thee away.
> Then I thy name shall magnify
>   And tell thy praise abroad,
> For very love and gladness I
>   Shall dance before my God.[13]

Such prayers and hymns as these must express, surely, diverse encounters with the same divine reality. These encounters have taken place within different human cultures by people of different ways of thought and feeling, with different histories and different frameworks of philosophical thought, and have developed into different systems of theology embodied in different religious structures and organisations. These resulting large-scale religio-cultural phenomena are what we call the religions of the world. But must there not lie behind them the same infinite divine reality, and may not our divisions into Christian, Hindu, Muslim, Jew, and so on, and all that goes with them, accordingly represent secondary, human, historical developments?

There is a further problem, however, which now arises. I have been speaking so far of the ultimate reality in a variety of terms—the Father, Son and Spirit of Christianity, the Jahweh of Judaism, the Allah of Islam, and so on—but always thus far in theistic terms, as a personal God under one name or another. But what of the non-theistic religions? What of the non-theistic Hinduism according to which the ultimate reality, Brahman, is not He but It; and what about Buddhism, which in one form is agnostic concerning the existence of God even though in another form it has come to worship the Buddha himself? Can these non-theistic faiths be seen as encounters with the same divine reality that is encountered in theistic religion?

Speaking very tentatively, I think it is possible that the sense of the divine as non-personal may indeed reflect an aspect of the same infinite reality that is encountered as personal in theistic religious experience. The question can be pursued both as a matter of pure theology and in relation to religious experience. Theologically, the Hindu distinction between Nirguna Brahman and Saguna Brahman is important and should be adopted into western religious thought. Detaching the distinction, then, from its Hindu context we may say that Nirguna God is the eternal self-existent divine reality, beyond the scope of all human categories, including personality; and Saguna God is God in relation to his creation and with the attributes which express this relationship, such as personality, omnipotence, goodness, love and omniscience. Thus the one ultimate reality is both Nirguna and non-personal, and Saguna and personal, in a duality which is in principle acceptable to human understanding. When we turn to men's religious awareness of God we are speaking of Saguna God, God in relation to man.

And here the larger traditions of both east and west report a dual experience of the divine as personal and as other than personal. It will be a sufficient reminder of the strand of personal relationship with the divine in Hinduism to mention Iswaru, the personal God who represents the Absolute as known and worshipped by finite persons. It should also be remembered that the characterisation of Brahman as *satcitananda*, absolute being, consciousness and bliss, is not far from the conception of infinitely transcendent personal life. Thus there is both the thought and the experience of the personal divine within Hinduism. But there is likewise the thought and the experience of God as other than personal within Christianity. Rudolph Otto describes this strand in the mysticism of Meister Eckhart. He says:

> The divine, which on the one hand is conceived in symbols taken from the social sphere, as Lord, King, Father, Judge—a person in relation to persons—is on the other hand denoted in dynamic symbols as the power of life, as light and life, as spirit ebbing and flowing, as truth, knowledge, essential justice and holiness, a glowing fire that penetrates and pervades. It is characterized as the principle of a renewed, supernatural Life, mediating and giving itself, breaking forth in the living man as his nova vita, as the content of his life and being. What is here insisted upon is not so much an immanent God as an "experienced" God, known as an inward principle of the power of new being and life. Eckhart knows this *deuteros theos* besides the personal God. . . .[14]

Let me now try to draw the threads together and to project them into the future. I have been suggesting that Christianity is a way of salvation which, beginning some two thousand years ago, has become the principal way of salvation in three continents. The other great faiths are likewise of salvation, providing the principal path to the divine reality for other large sections of humanity. I have also suggested that the idea that Jesus proclaimed himself as God incarnate, and as the sole point of saving contact between God and man, is without adequate historical foundation and represents a doctrine developed by the church. We should therefore not infer, from the Christian experience of redemption through Christ, that salvation cannot be experienced in any other way. The alternative possibility is that the ultimate divine reality—in our Christian terms, God—has always been pressing in upon the human spirit, but in ways which leave men free to open or close themselves to the divine presence. Human life has developed along characteristically different lines in the main areas of civilisation, and these differences have naturally entered into the ways in which men have apprehended and responded to God. For the great religious figures through whose experience divine revelation has come have each been conditioned by a particular history and culture. One can hardly imagine Gotama the Buddha except in the setting of the India of his time, or Jesus the Christ except against the background of Old Testament Judaism, or Mohammed except in the setting of Arabia. And human history and culture have likewise shaped the development of the webs of religious creeds, practices and organisations which we know as the great world faiths.

It is thus possible to consider the hypothesis that they are all, at their experiential roots, in contact with the same ultimate reality, but that their differing experiences of that reality, interacting over the centuries with the different thought-forms of different cultures, have led to increasing differentiation and contrasting elaboration—so that Hinduism, for example, is a very different phenomenon from Christianity, and very different ways of conceiving and experiencing the divine occur within them.

However, now that the religious traditions are consciously interacting with each other in the "one world" of today, in mutual observation and dialogue, it is possible that their future developments may be on gradually converging courses. For during the next few centuries they will no doubt continue to change, and it may be that they will grow closer together, and even that one day such names as "Christianity," "Buddhism," "Islam," "Hinduism," will no longer describe the then current configurations of men's religious experience and belief. I am not here thinking of the extinction of human religiousness in a universal wave of secularisation. This is of course a possible future; and indeed many think it the most likely future to come about. But if man is an indelibly religious animal he will always, even in his secular cultures, experience a sense of the transcendent by which he will be both troubled and uplifted. The future I am thinking of is accordingly one in which what we now call the different religions will constitute the past history of different emphases and variations within a global religious life. I do not mean that all men everywhere will be overtly religious, any more than they are today. I mean rather that the discoveries now taking place by men of different faiths of central common ground, hitherto largely concealed by the variety of cultural forms in which it was expressed, may eventually render obsolete the sense of belonging to rival ideological communities. Not that all religious men will think alike, or worship in the same way or experience the divine identically. On the contrary, so long as there is a rich variety of human cultures—and let us hope there will always be this—we should expect there to be correspondingly different forms of religious cult, ritual and organisation, conceptualised in different theological doctrines. And so long as there is a wide spectrum of human psychological types—and again let us hope that there will always be this—we should expect there to be correspondingly different emphases between, for example, the sense of the divine as just and as merciful, between *karma* and *bhakti*; or between worship as formal and communal and worship as free and personal. Thus we may expect the different world faiths to continue as religio-cultural phenomena, though phenomena which are increasingly influencing one another's development. The relation between them will then perhaps be somewhat like that now obtaining between the different denominations of Christianity in Europe or the United States. That is to say, there will in most countries be a dominant religious tradition, with other traditions present in varying strengths, but with considerable awareness on all hands of what they have in common; with some degree of osmosis of membership through their institutional walls; with a large degree of practical cooperation; and even conceivably with some interchange of ministry.

Beyond this the ultimate unity of faiths will be an eschatological unity in which each is both fulfilled and transcended—fulfilled in so far as it is true, transcended in so far as it is less than the whole truth. And indeed even such fulfilling must be a transcending; for the function of a religion is to bring us to a right relationship with the ultimate divine reality, to awareness of our true nature and our place in the Whole, into the presence of God. In the eternal life there is no longer any place for religions; the pilgrim has no need of a way after he has finally arrived. In St. John's vision of the heavenly city at the end of our Christian scriptures it is said that there is no temple—no Christian church or chapel, no Jewish synagogue, no Hindu or Buddhist temple, no Muslim mosque, no Sikh gurdwara. . . . For all these exist in time, as ways through time to eternity.

Notes

1. *Elements of Social Organization*, 3rd ed. (London: Tavistock Publications, 1969) p. 216.

2. *The Meaning and End of Religion* (New York: Mentor Books, 1963) p. 22.

3. *A History of Religion East and West* (London: Macmillan and New York: St. Martin's Press, 1968) p. 27.

4. The dating of the Bhagavad Gītā has been a matter of much

debate; but R. C. Zaehner in his recent monumental critical edition says that "One would probably not be going far wrong if one dated it as some time between the fifth and second centuries B.C." *The Bhagavad Gītā* (Oxford: Clarendon Press, 1969) p. 7.

5. I 164.

6 IV II.

7. Kenneth Cragg, *Alive to God: Muslim and Christian Prayer* (London and New York: Oxford University Press, 1970) p. 65.

8. Harbans Singh, *Guru Nanak and Origins of the Sikh Faith* (Bombay, London and New York: Asia Publishing House, 1969), pp. 96–97.

9. *Alive to God*, p. 61 (Surah of the Kneeling, v. 35).

10. *Sacred Books of the World*, edited by A. C. Bouquet (London: Pelican Books, 1954) p. 226 (The Rāmāyana of Tulsi Das, Canto 1, Chandha 2, translated by F. S. Growse).

11. Ibid., p. 245 (A Hymn of Namdev, translated by Nicol Mac-Nicol).

12. *Alive to God*, p. 79 (From Ibn Hazm, "The Ring of the Dove").

13. *Sacred Books of the World*, p. 246 (A Hymn of Tukaram).

14. Rudolph Otto, *Mysticism East and West*, trans. Bertha L. Bracey and Richenda C. Payne (New York: Meridian Books, 1957), p. 131.

INDEX